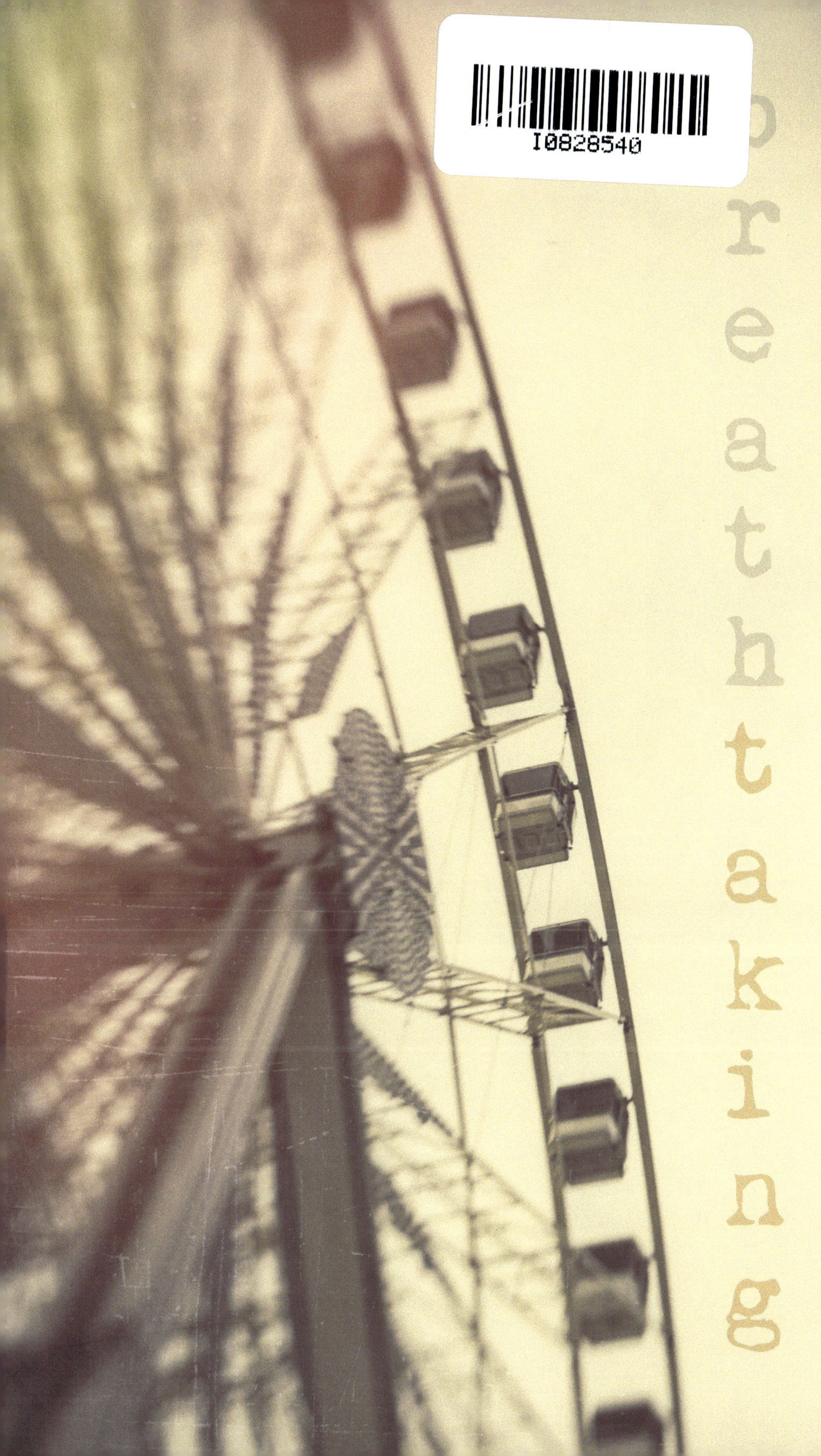

breathtaking

breathtaking
the language of pause

susan currie

shanti arts publishing
brunswick, maine

breathtaking
the language of pause

published by shanti arts publishing
designed by shanti arts designs

shanti arts llc
193 hillside road
brunswick, maine 04011
www.shantiarts.com

printed in the united states of america

isbn: 978-1-947067-91-2 (softcover)

library of congress control number: 2019943436

repurposes

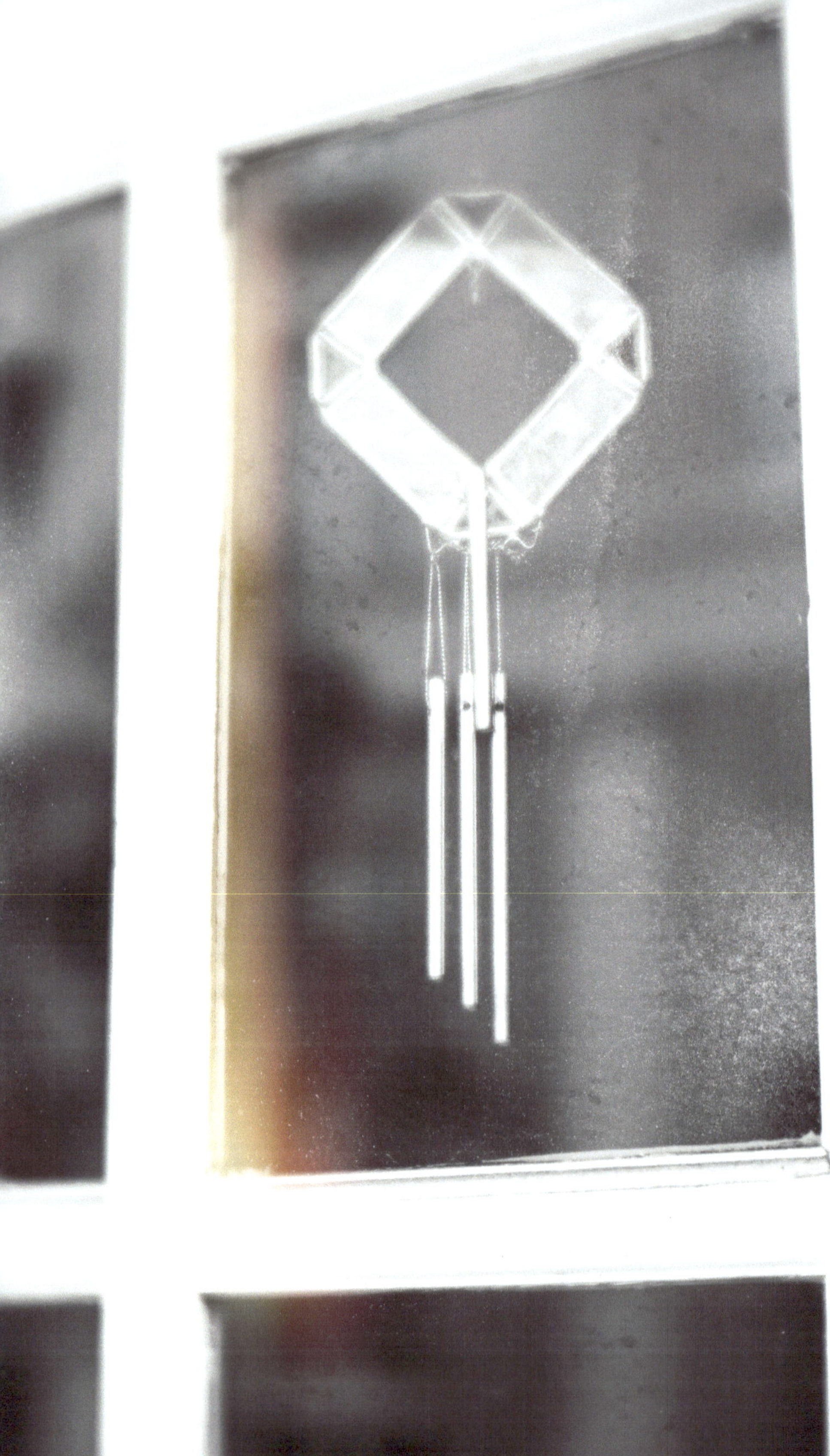

a great big "namaste" to all of the willing
who step in front of my lens and offer a
bit of their light. i am ever grateful
to each of you and to the kindred spirits
who share this intention to counter the
chaos and live life more fully present.

i would especially like to thank my publisher
christine cote for her ongoing interest
in my work and for daring to nudge the
margins of how poetic verse is served up.

to my teaching partner and longtime pal joyce
tenneson, it is my privilege to work with you.

to my parents, much love and
thanks for all that you do.

and to david, hannah and max...
this one is (also) for you.

fade far away, dissolve and quite forget
what thou among the leaves has never known,
the weariness, the fever, and the fret
-john keats

the language of pause - i have long been charmed by its infinite translations. as a result, in my work as a photographer and writer, i find myself holding a prism up in study of the assorted manners in which we as a culture "dissolve." well beyond the confines of any framed views, **inhales and exhales take the shape that they will**. gently probing gestures and instances in which we as a culture subtract ourselves from the grid of life and then setting my photographs to lyrics, my intent is to reflect back some truths of the mosaic of practices in service of breathing.

these pages which follow serve as my aria to (and reminder of) those simple glories which truly nourish the soul. may they serve as a **quiet reminder** of the beauty available to us in every moment. here's to our fade aways...whatever the manner, now more than ever.

-susan currie

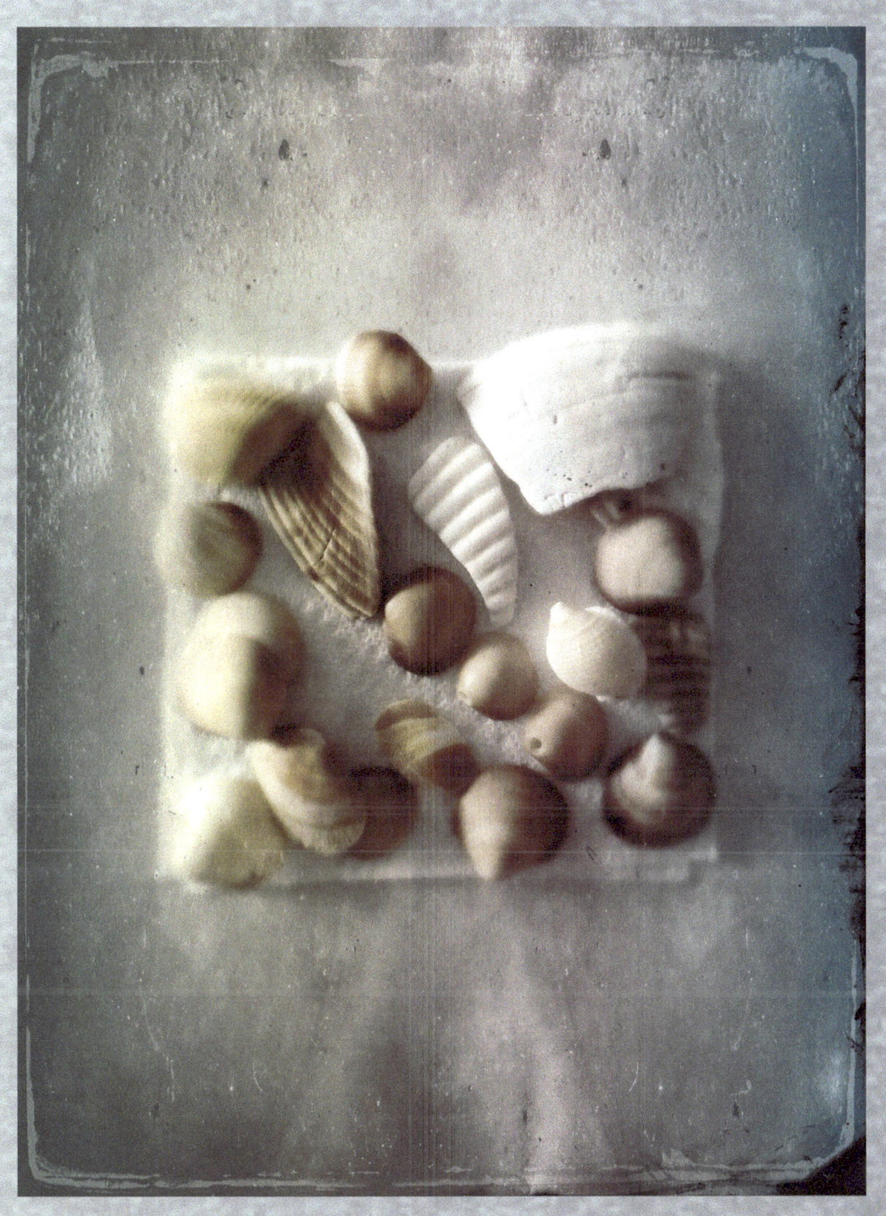

trimming

"the boat that you build...
make upper and lower decks.
the tackle must be very strong,
the bitumen strong,
to give it strength..."

sometimes i remember...
trimming man's noisy behavior can
be accomplished

without
shears

many worlds exist in a small room
we are welcome
to access them all
or, to range freely

order spans among the construction site

go see for yourself
what beautiful looks like

make steady your course
in the silent pocket
the noise points the way

i
n
t
e
n
t
i
o
n

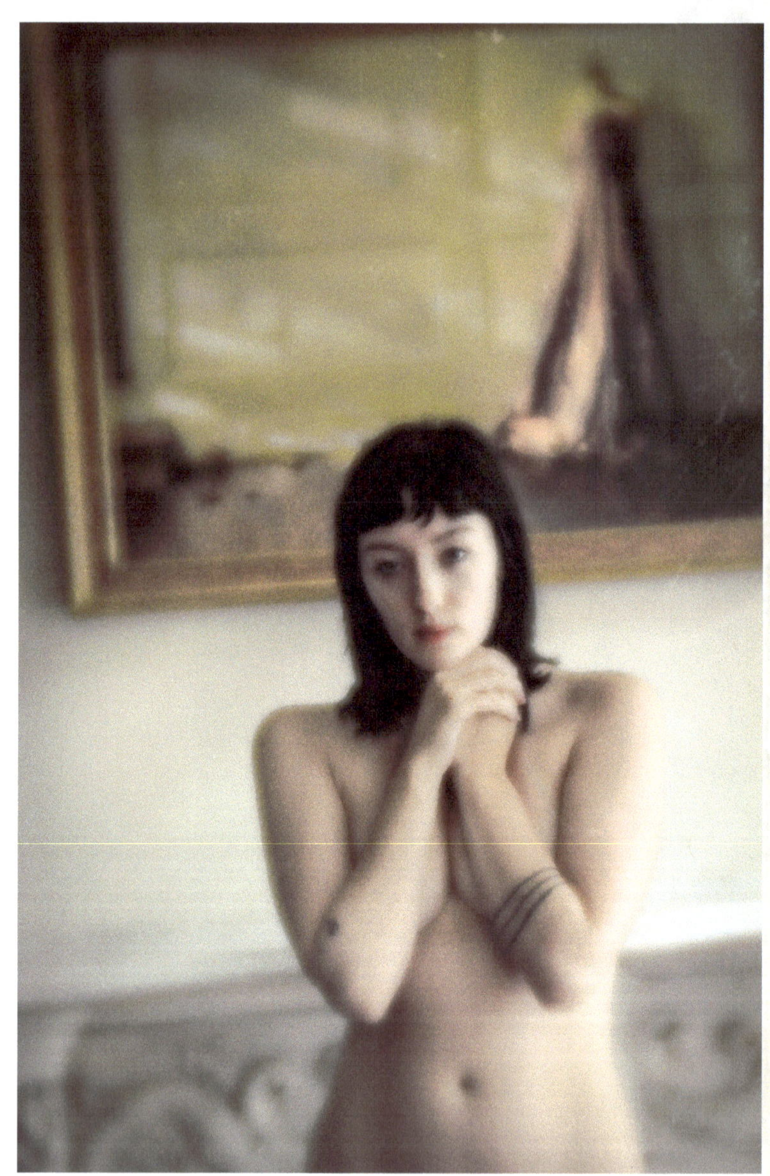

be me
be you
be the one

be curiosity, be color
be the force field

be composition
be silence,
and be song

be, be, be
the pulse

be, be, be
the one

NOTE

profile views

neighbor
student
worker
render
thinker
writer
observer

the sum of seven was he

"is not the poet bound to write
his own biography?"

ever new
every day
look up, look up

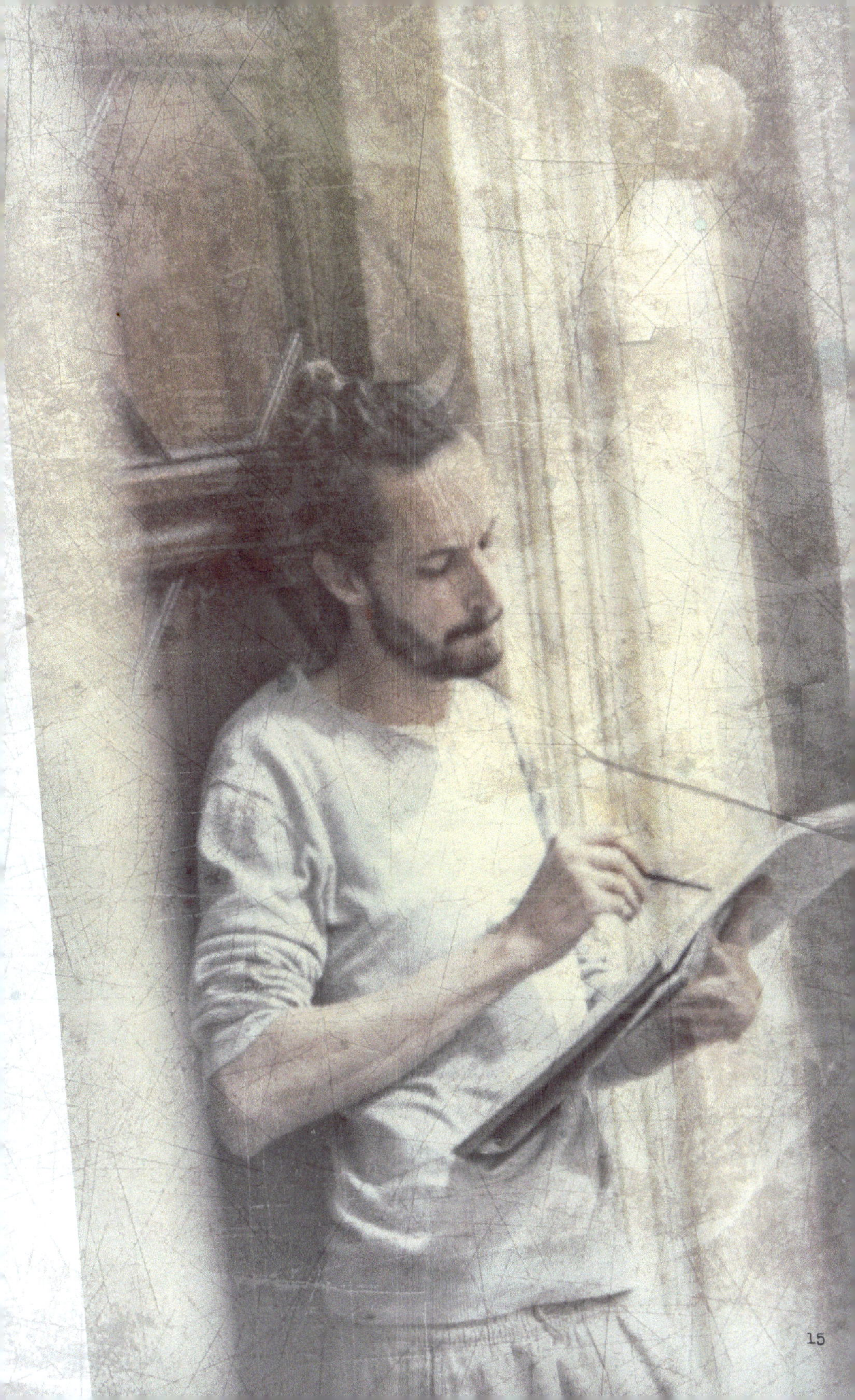

austerities

on the downward slope
from the thirsty incline
from the thorns, glances at me

a burgundy bloom

through the battered shutters
of my darkened hillside quarters
   sails this beacon
with no hesitations

its simplicity, in shadow

   a clue
   that my bothers
   may ebb

whatever their dimension,
whenever they will
such movements
such movements

hours later, poise again

then an aisle
  in the expanse
of rolling hills

JE ME SOUVIENS

ADMIT ONE
FREEZE, EMPTY
REST, RETURN

OMIT NONE
STILL, GATHER,
REPOSE, RESUME

COUNTING CHIMES AND LOSING COUNT
CLIMBING HILLS IN SEARCH OF ROSES

AS IF THERE WERE...
NO WRONG TURN
HERE

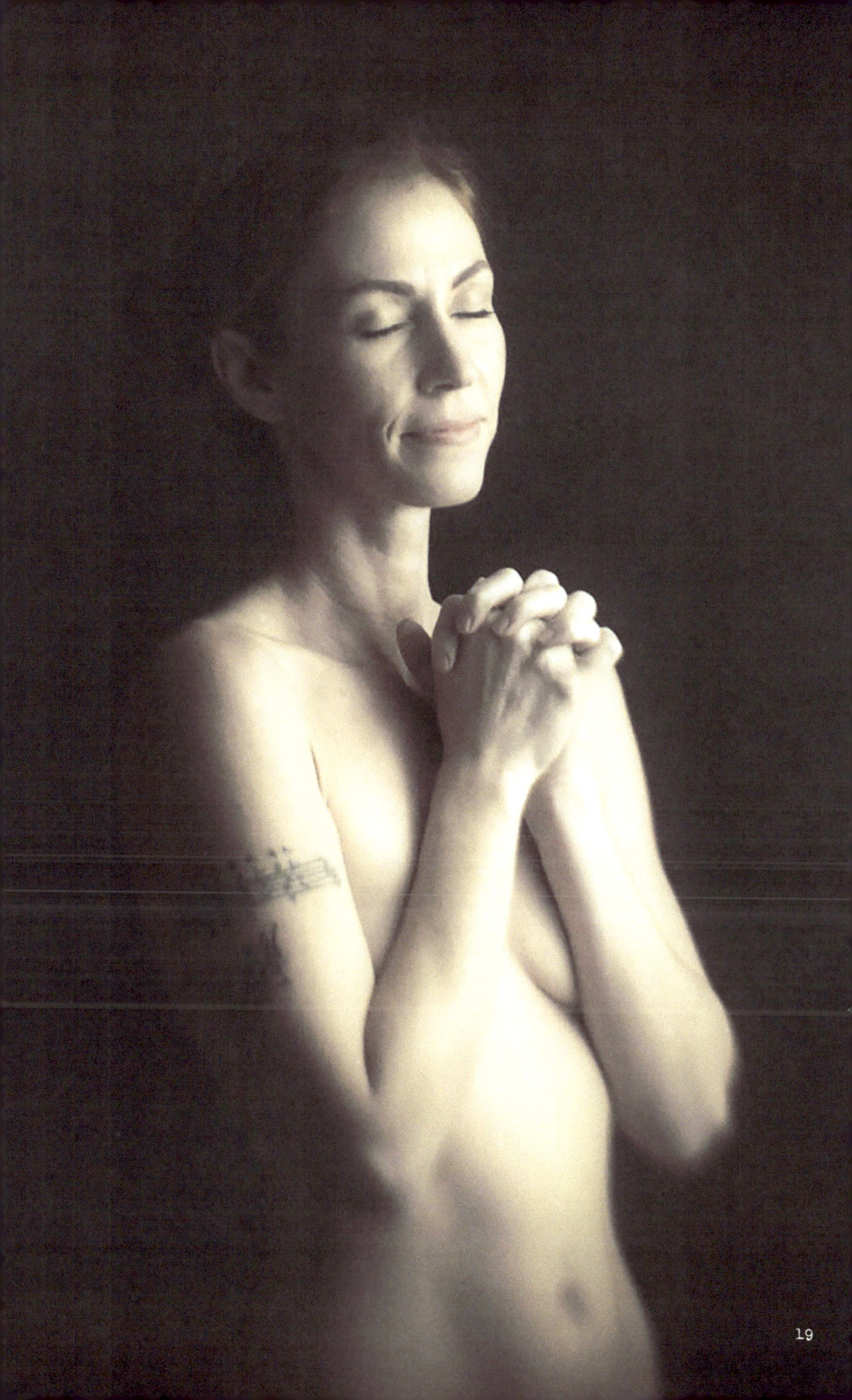

inhal

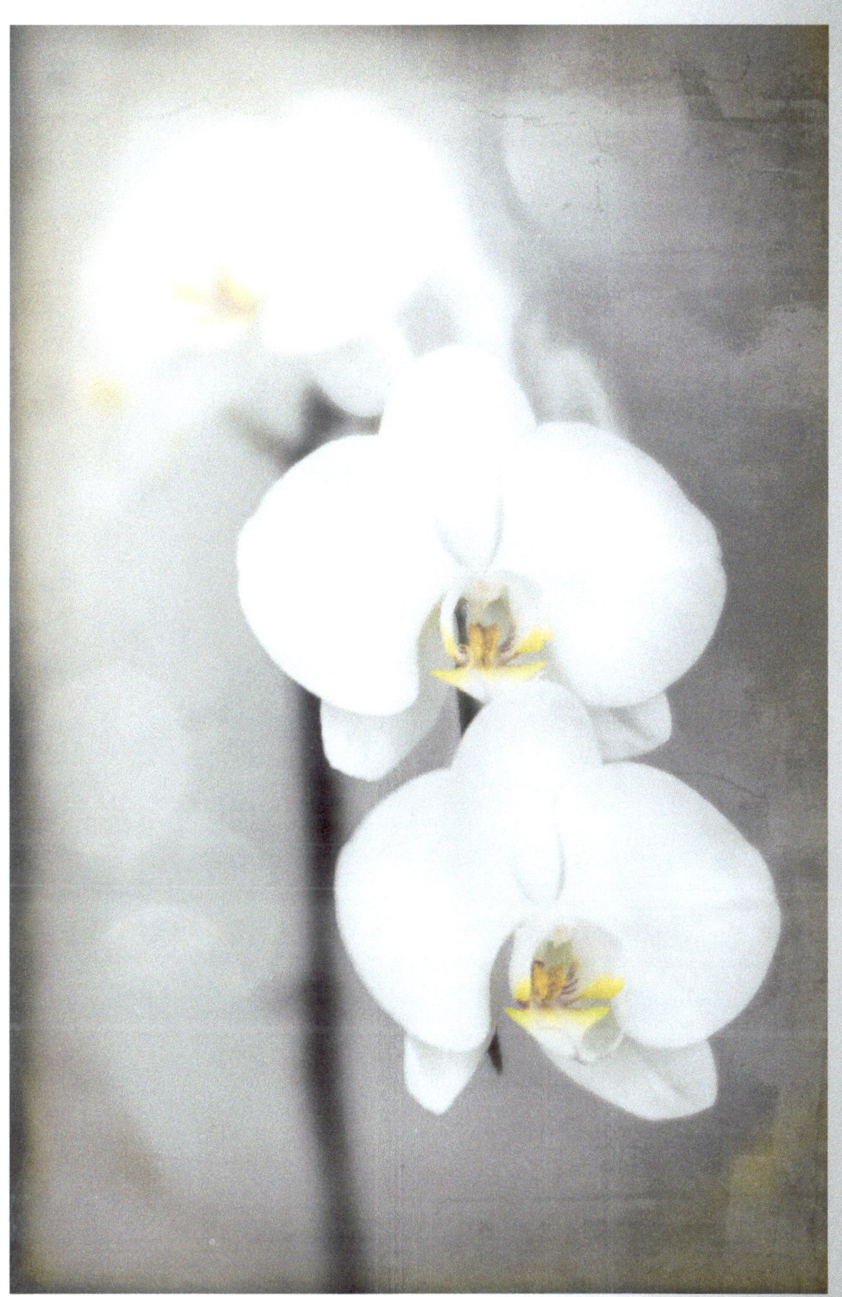

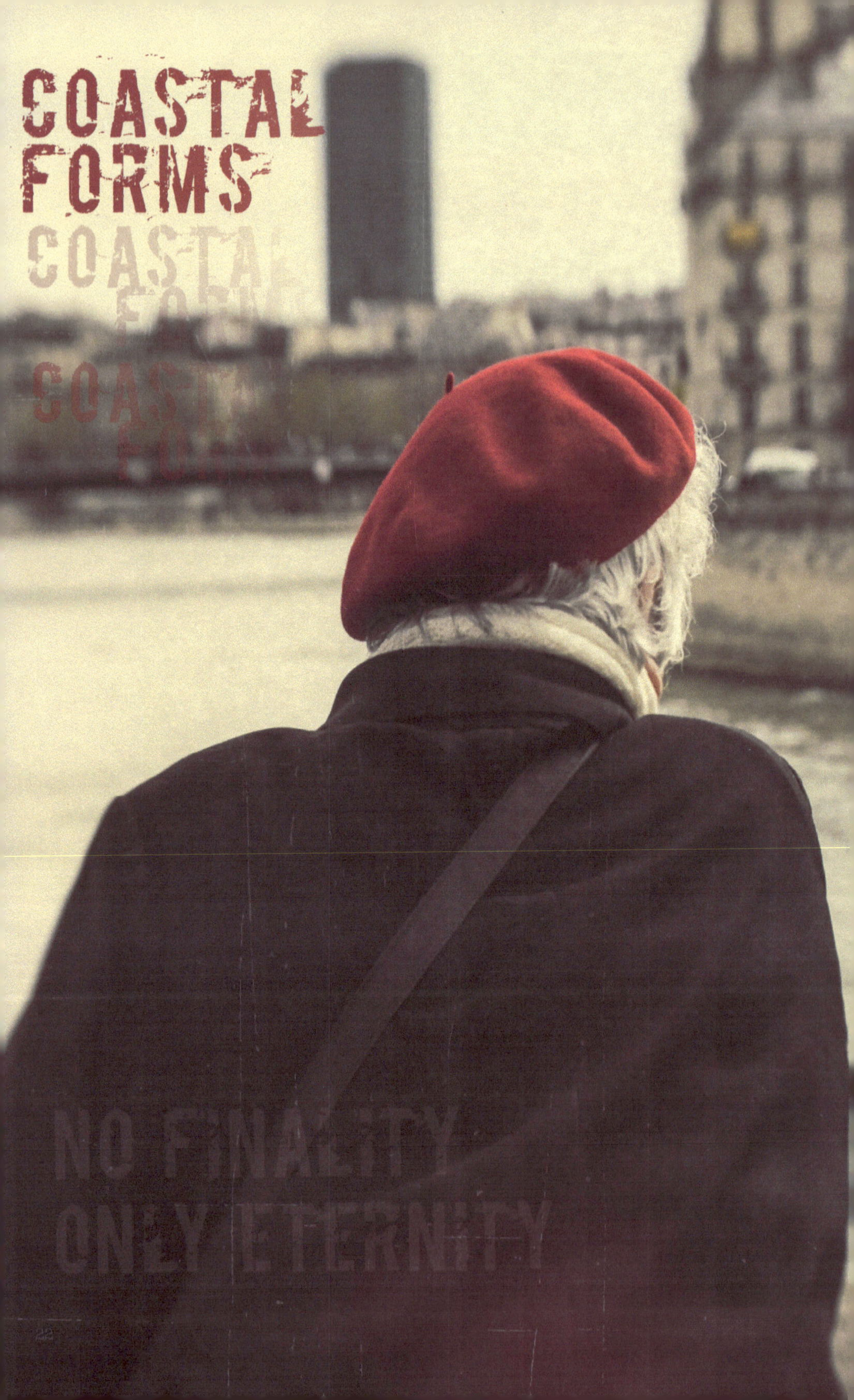

COASTAL FORMS

NO FINALITY
ONLY ETERNITY

and now i narrate thyself
just this one

so go the moments lived
...quietly
in the searchlight

it would be easy to confuse this as
inaction
   but the truth is

practice and practice and back
flash
to rewind
and then,
      practice again

     the truth is
     it's a different move
     move
     move
     move

          sound and vision
          space and resource
          omitting none
          ah jasmine

rise and recede
over and over
and then,
                rest
                in a new
                shoreline
                like the surf

          no finality
          only eternity

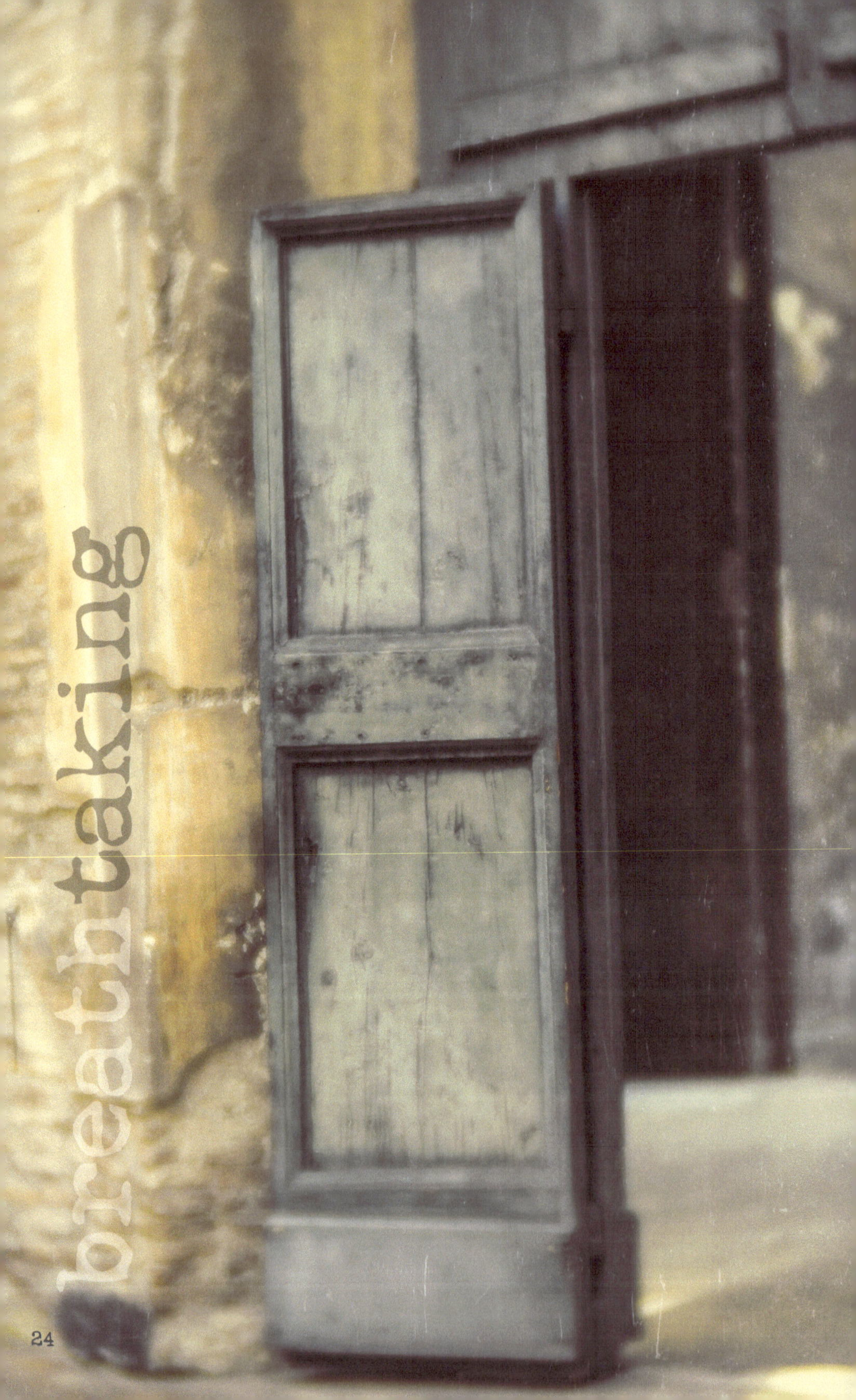
breathtaking

breathtaking

ME, GO, YES

in dreams i was a circle
rotating high
circumference, ME

waiting on the bus
i wanted to be
the ride
revolutions
over and under
and again

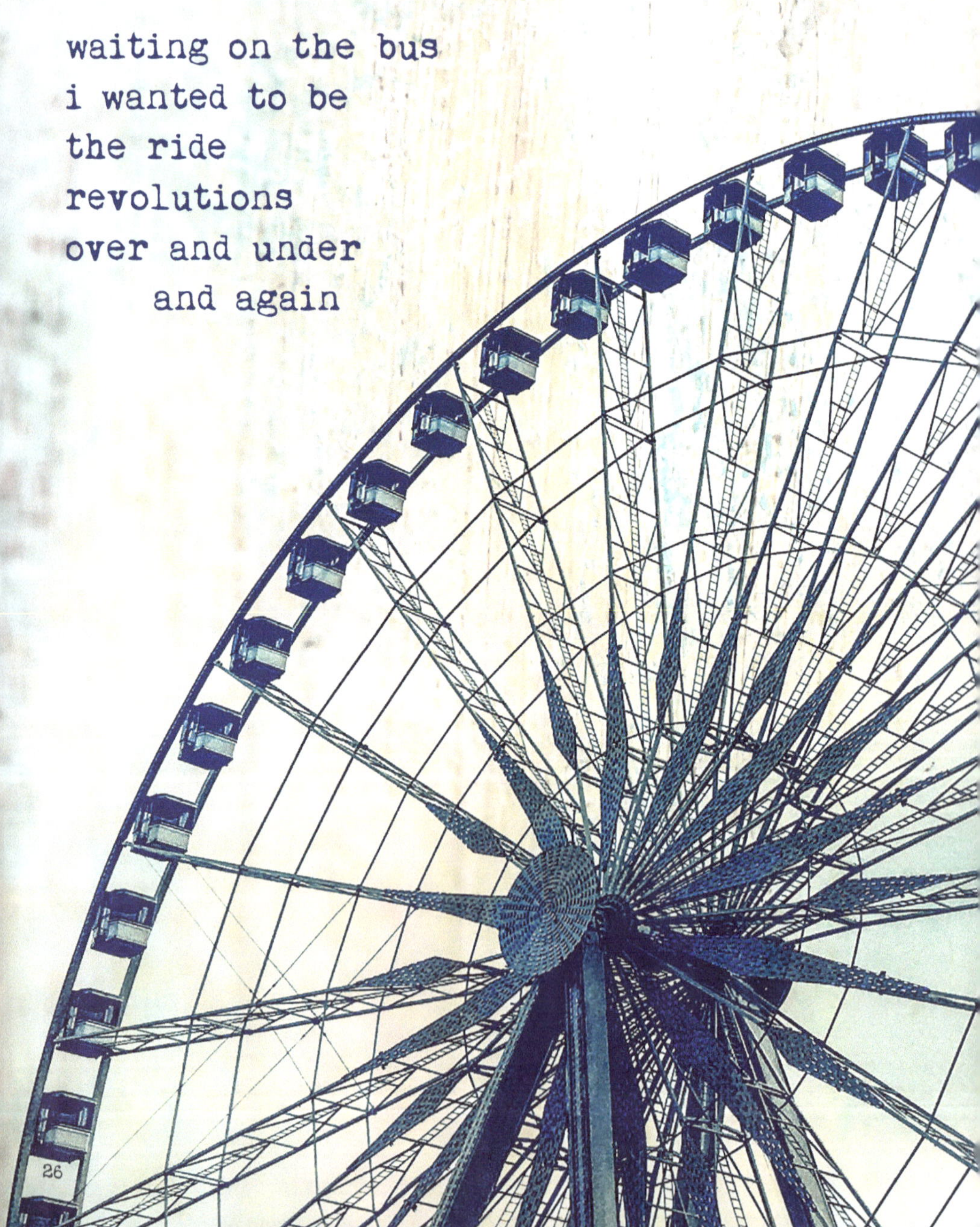

back then, the wind blew
the fanfare was me
twirling and possible,
and bound for
galaxies

when **GO** was my compass
the wheel i was
palms to pavements
spilling revolutions
speaking the
language
of

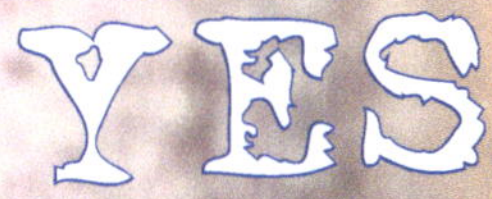

go majestic

outside in, inside out
in gestures of transparency,
there's a moment where i *GO*

i'm *ENDLESSLY* interested in this one
who resembles me
her wandering ways
some days comporting with reverence
and on others,
an air of the sinister

she has songs in there
INSIDE OUT, OUTSIDE IN,
ONLY LIGHT

today, i am the magnet
the author
and choreographer
and director
curious and calling
on my self
to go majestic

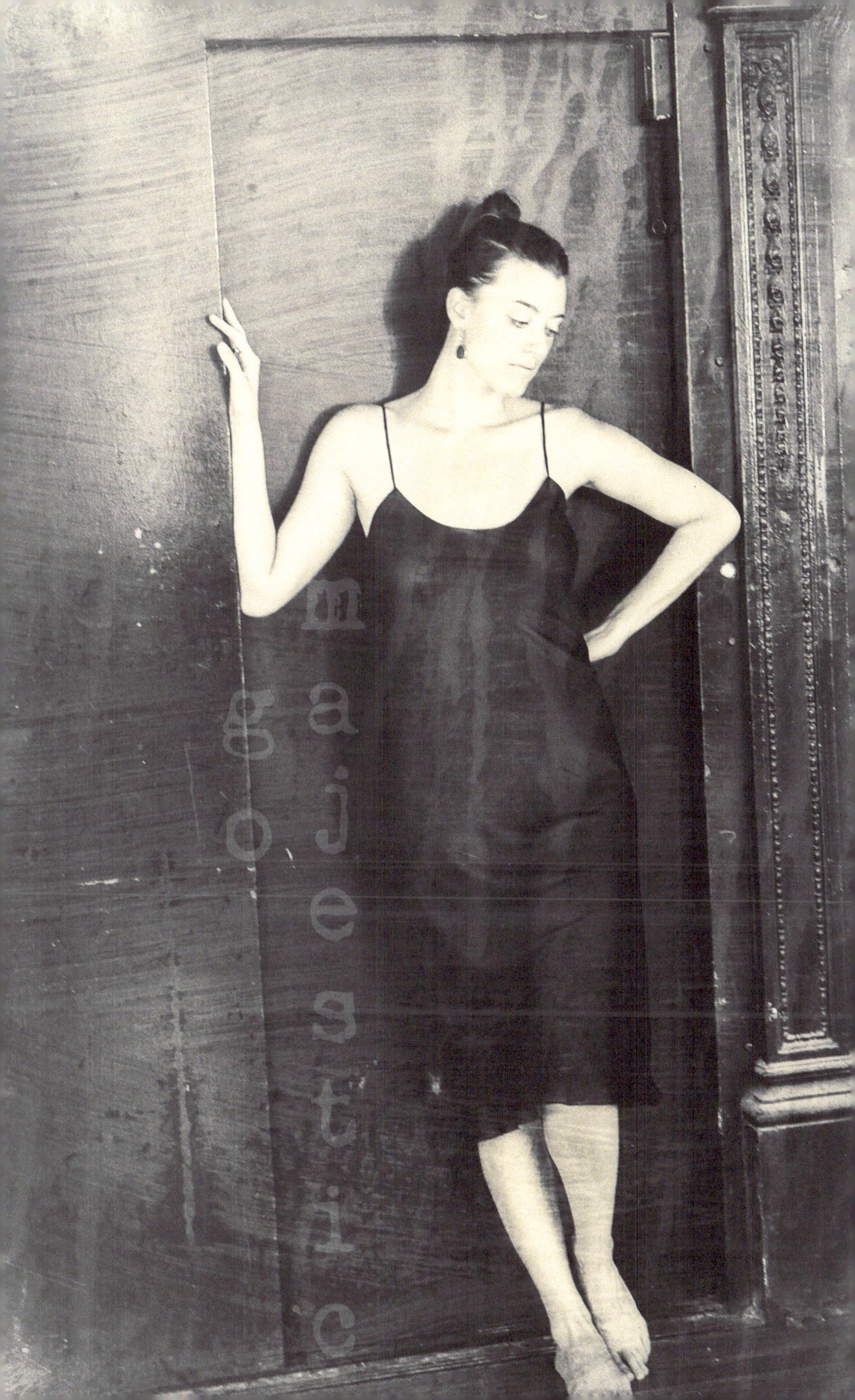
majestic
go

breathtaking

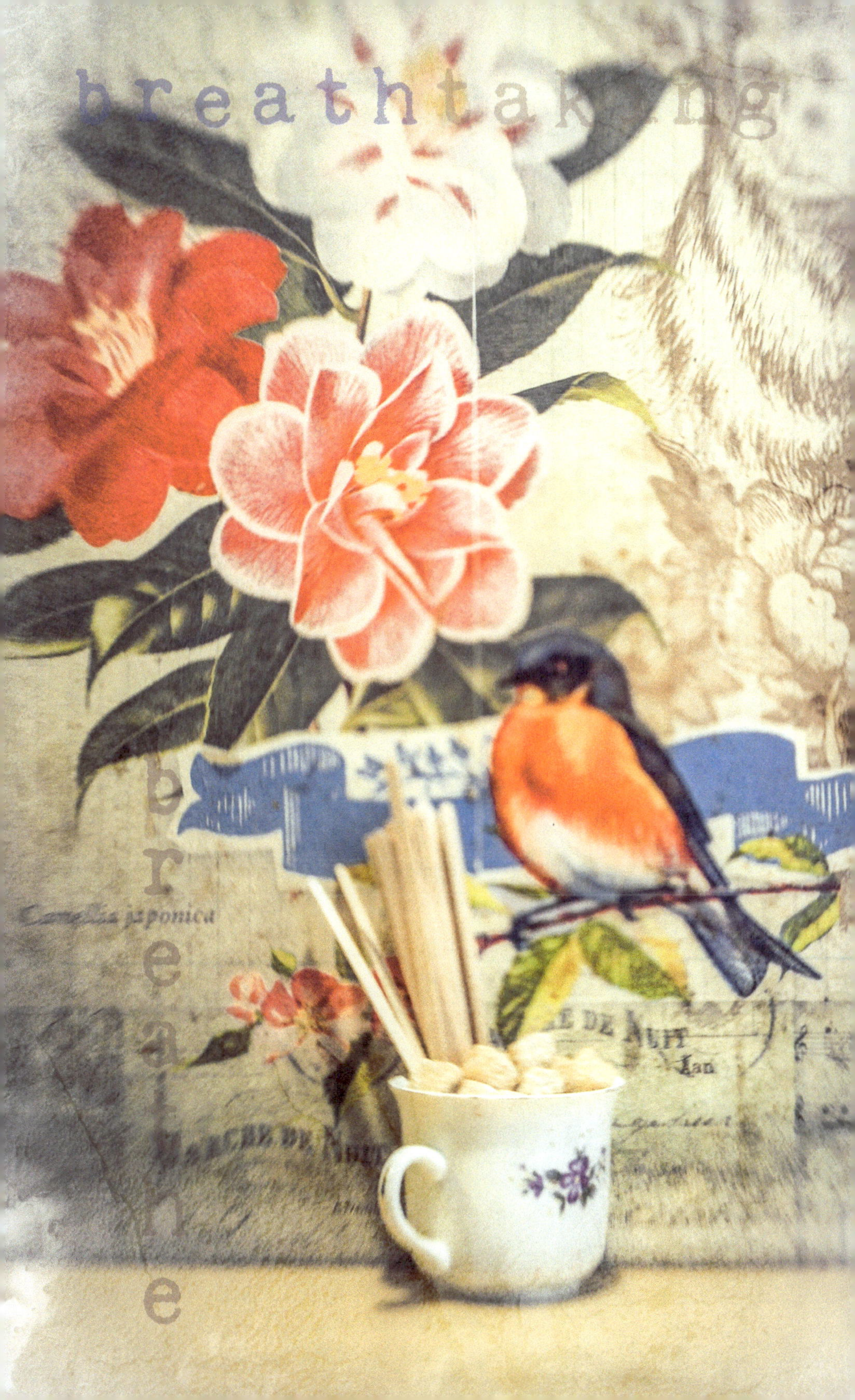

breathtaking

breathe

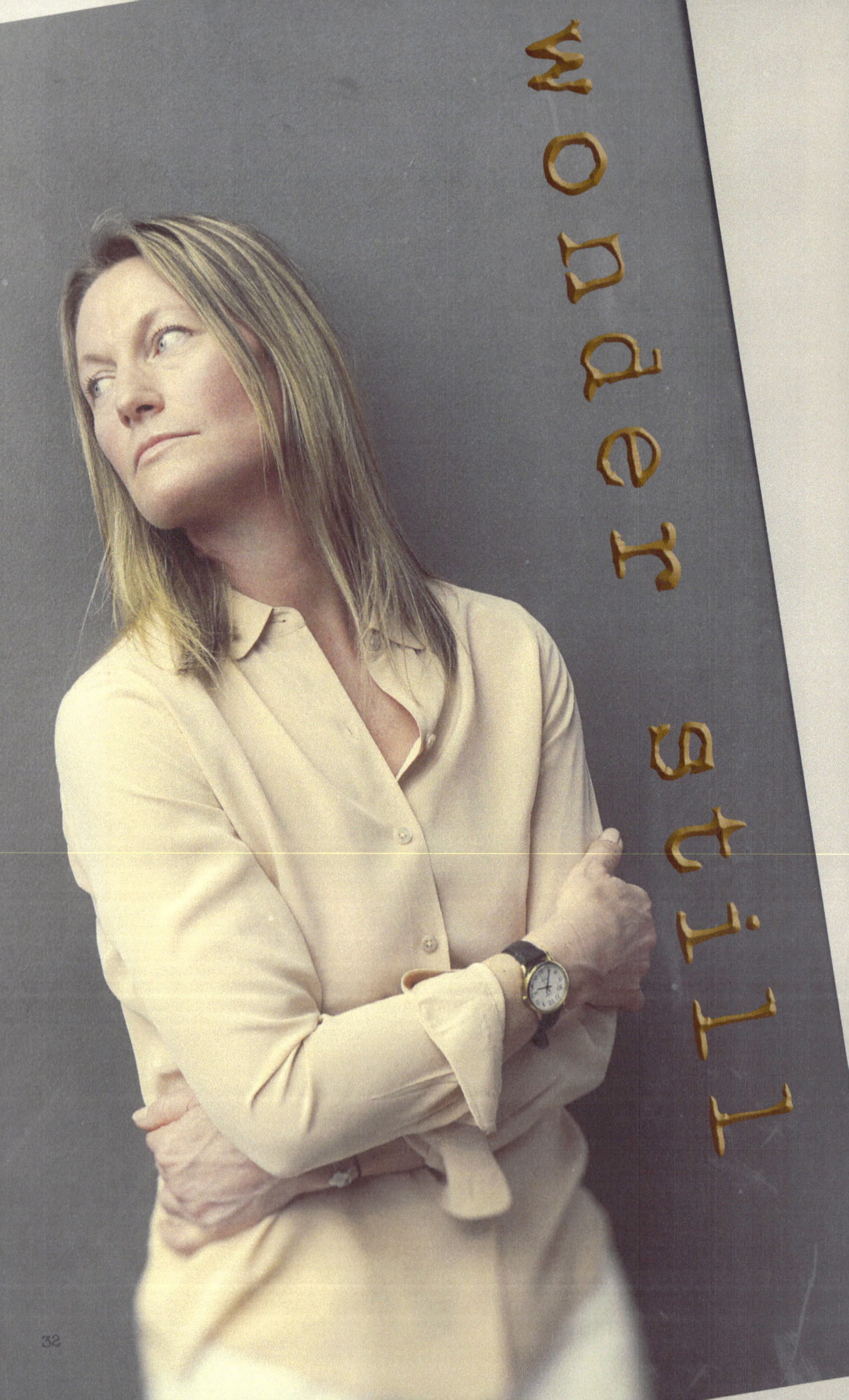
wonder still

as i sit here
at the world's bedside
i wonder . . .
to whom is this happening
the slaughter, the flooding,
the falsehoods
and the overlooking
of one another

why does my my heart ache so?

why the sadness

and tomorrow, as i sit
sit at the earth's bedside
i will wonder still
to whom is this happening
the bluest sky
stream and rivers rippling
the shrub burning crimson

why does my my heart ache so?

why the joy

groundwork

urgent for me now is breath
ambitious inhales and gently roaming releases,
which transport me to
    empty

as a field of silence drapes over my lids,
illumination visits
with this mouth hushed, humility pools
through vacant ears, answers
report

a blanket of reverence drapes
as the forage extends to weary limbs
let me do the math?

urgent for me now are corridors into silence
to its flood
where spaciousness, where spirit,
where succor umbrella
where all is quiet for once,
but for the richness itself of now

some days, in my travels
to the land of enough
a say in the matter filters the pelt
brushstrokes disguised as strangers

I have a poem
holy, holy, holy
lurks in quests of gentle currency

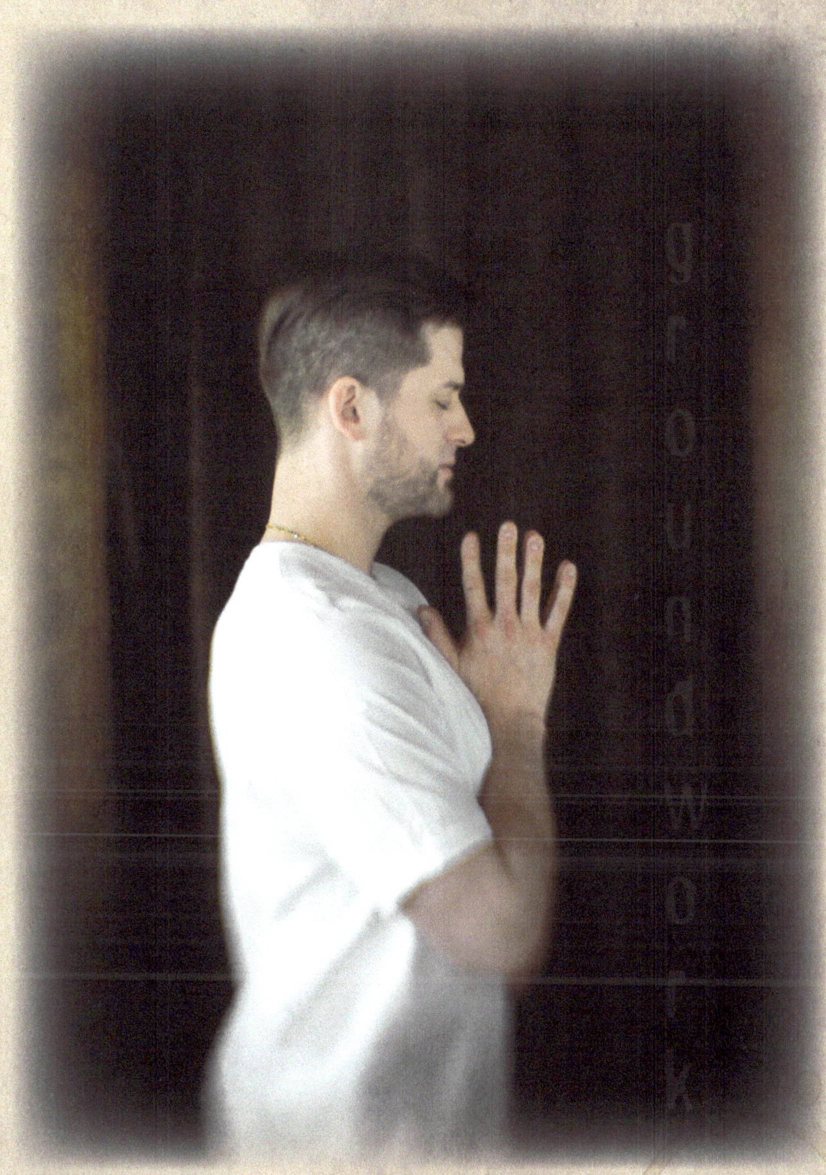
groundwork

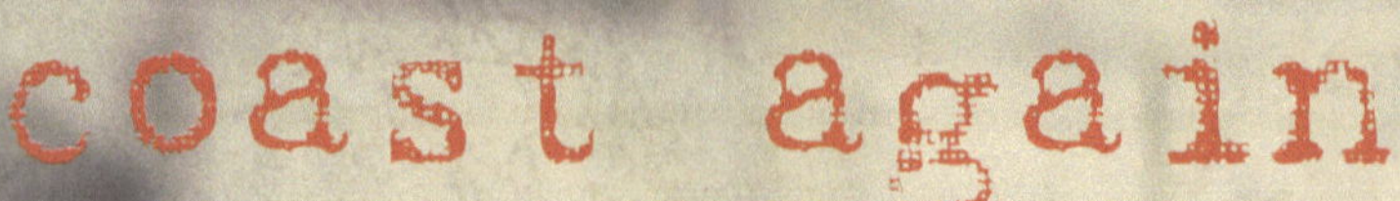

can someone
please
just put the training wheels
back
on?

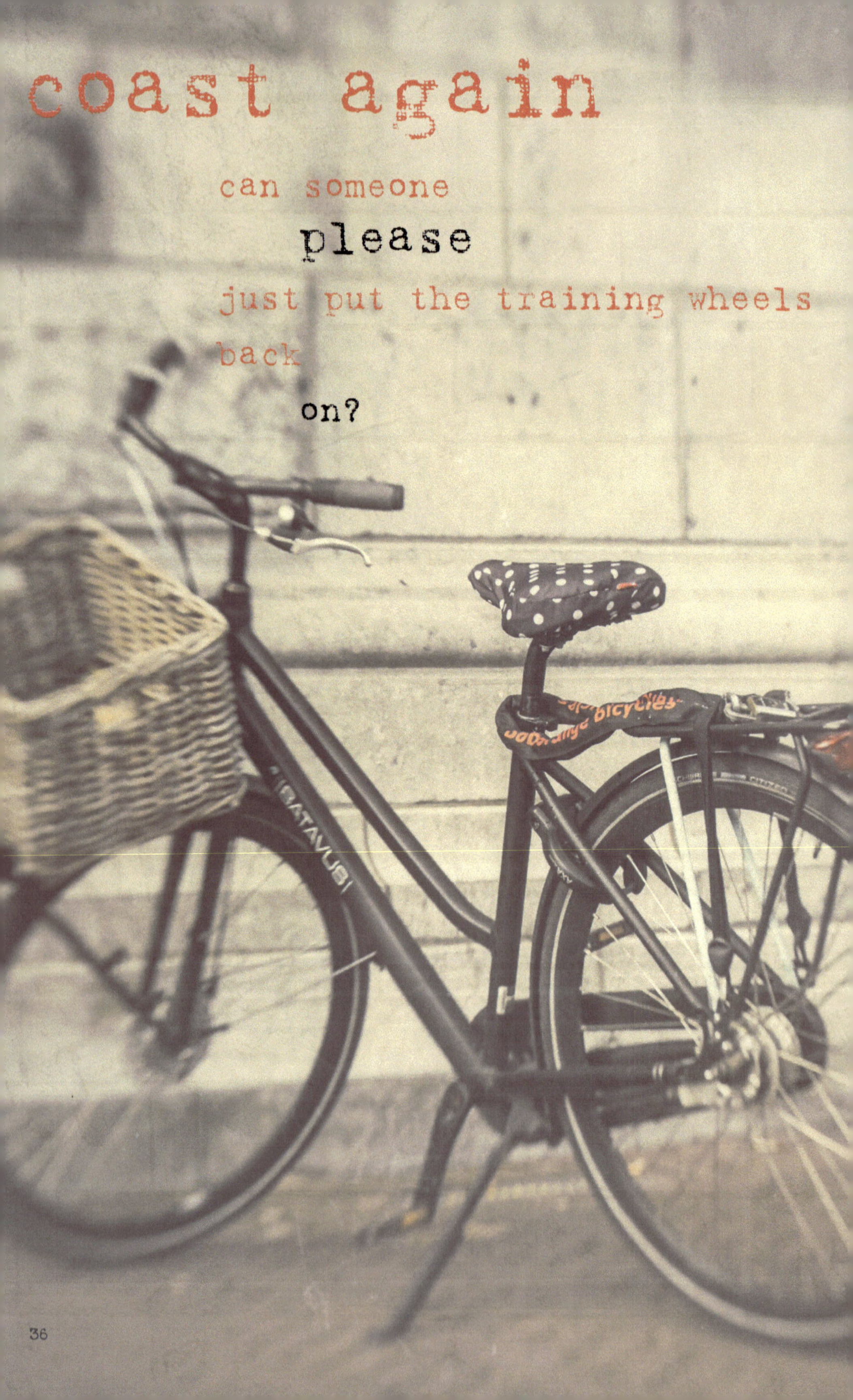

i want to coast again

through januarys and julys
my unabridged self
spirit flashing

i want to just GO
green light through the wind
let the secondary shoulder the concern
of tipping
over

in lunchbox days
go was
just that
forward

the days breathing me

i'm calling out for backup
so i might again pedal
green light through the wind,
so that i might please
coast
and be

free

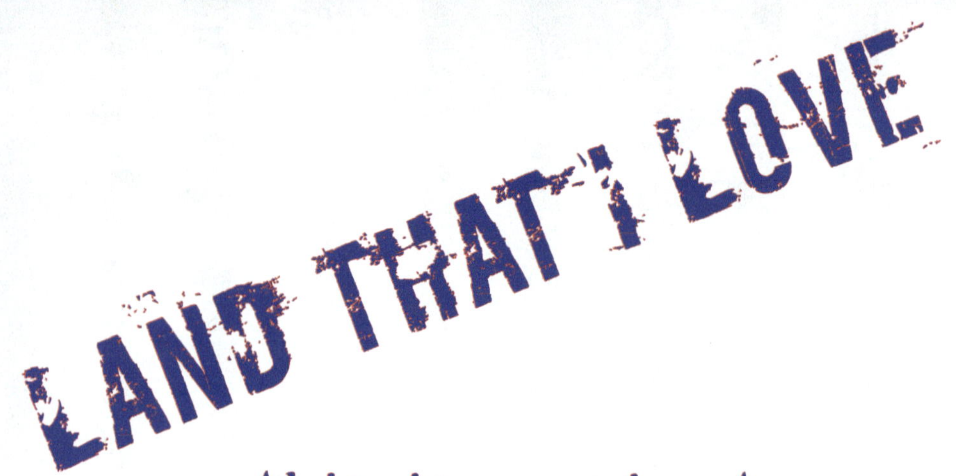

this is america to me

on a saturday summer
with the fog ghosting the shore
and this old house
letting it

to me,
this is america

the privilege

to act on impulse

follow my bliss

to pull the car off at the marsh's edge

the privilege to hop out, at magic time

and make myself a picture

tomorrow, and the next
it will reveal itself in
new ways
this land

but for today

i know just this definition

at dusk

in the seascape

outside the clam shack

...grace shed

WITNESS

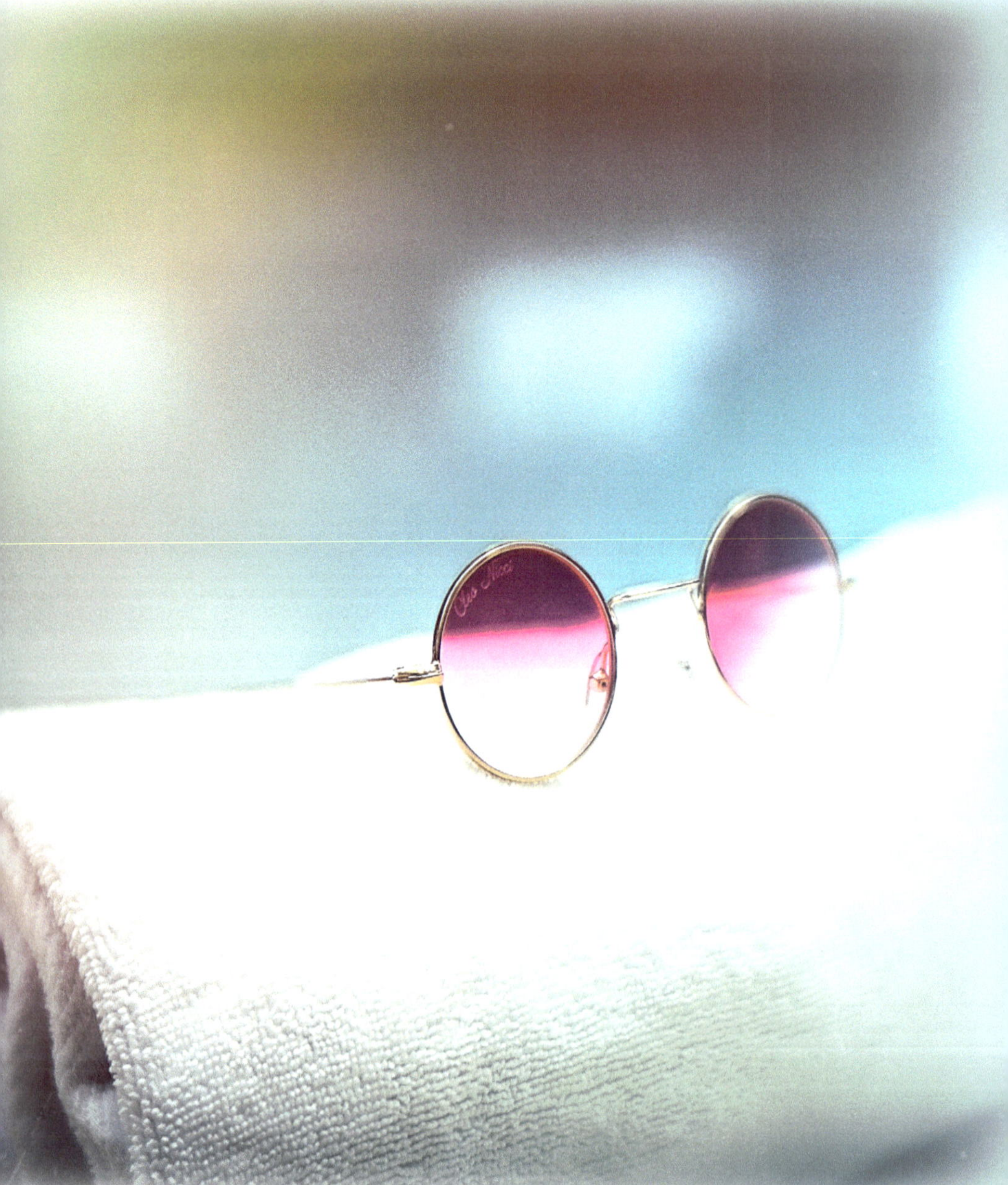

monday morning
the cherry striped chaises sit empty
umbrellas idle

all is hushed
just you and i
face to face

you roar in and over
and out
again and again
no time to lose

you roar in
over and out
cleansing the shore
of the weekend's racket,
preparing for the new

just you and i for some moments
shoulder to shoulder
in the champagne air

and, what i can do
what i can do - the only thing
is to offer my silence, my truest
perception
prayer like
in awe
of your
ministry

movements

perhaps
happiness is
just this
breathing in,
breathing out
and again
and again

only this
releasing the notes faintly
as they arrive and recede,
when they arrive and recede

not them, not there, not it
not yesterday, nor saturday
just this, only this

again and again

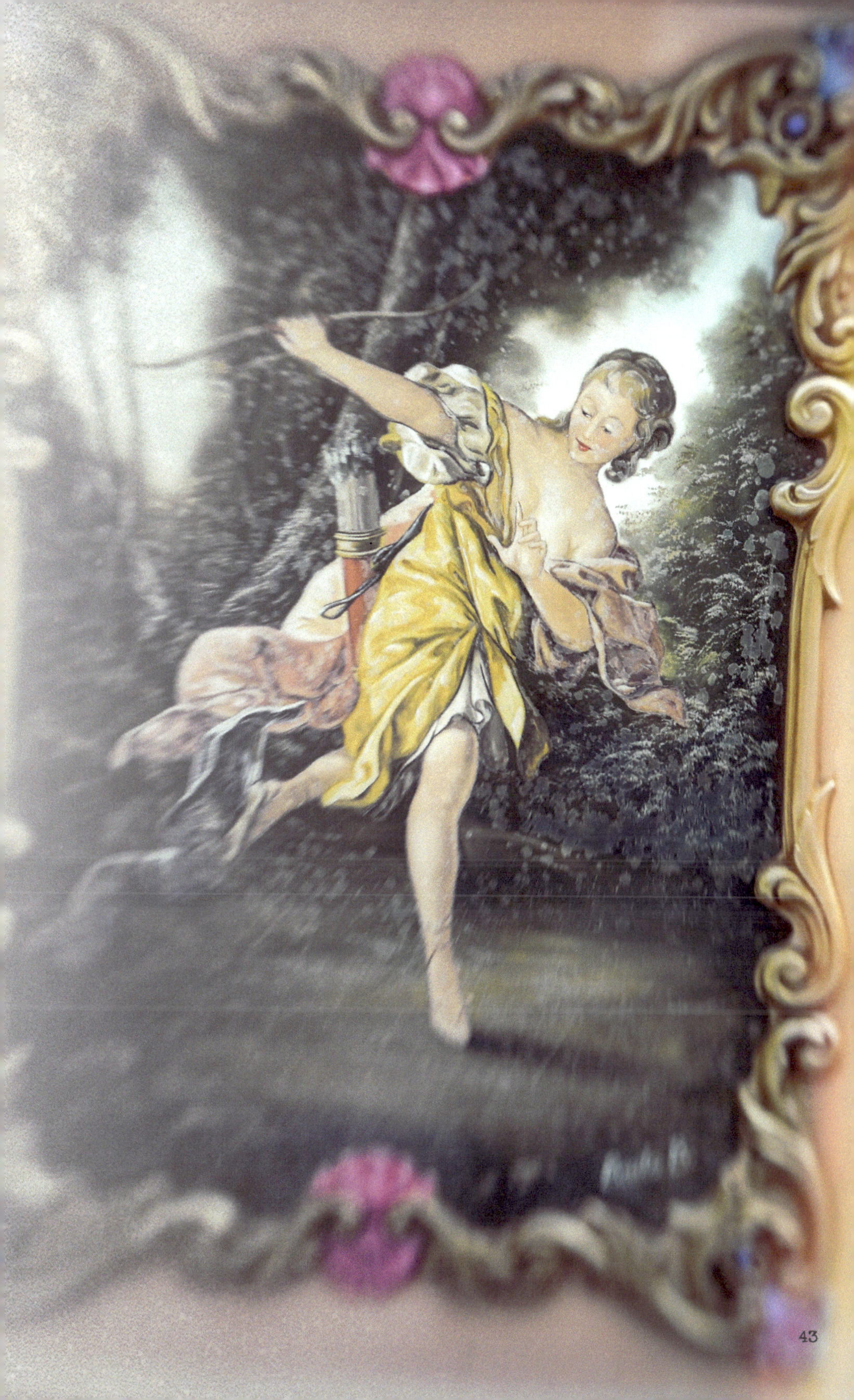

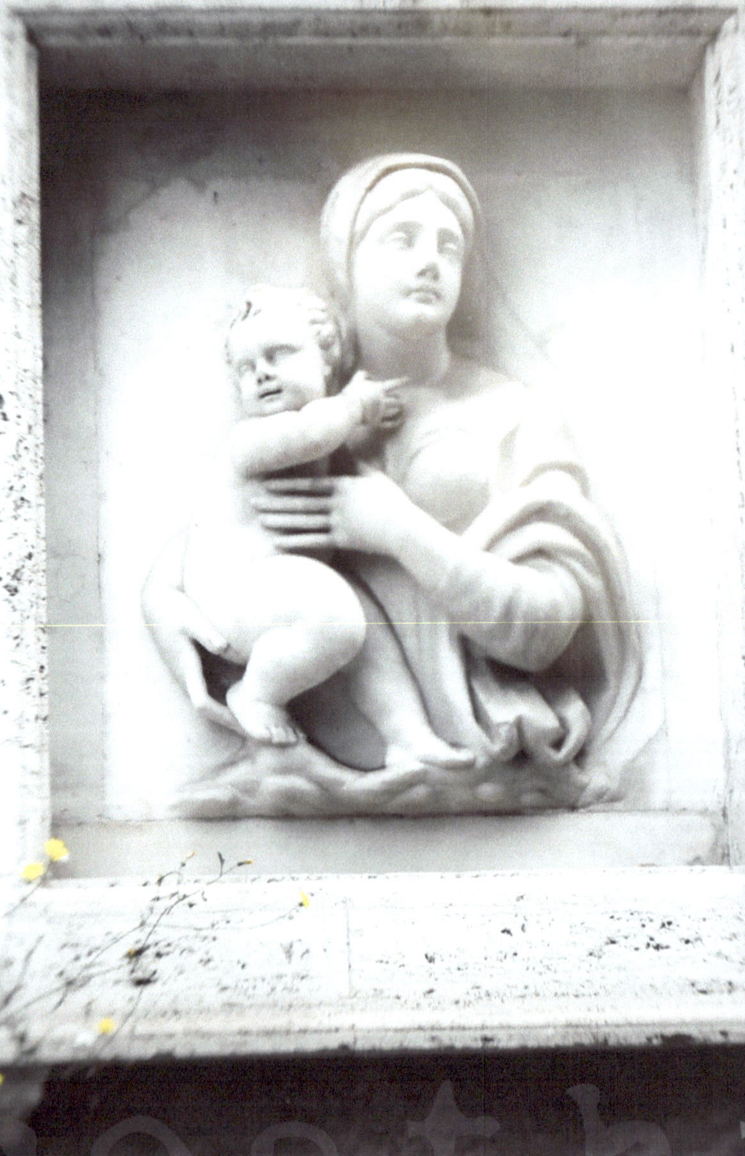

breath

breathtaking

aking

the throughline

where is east?
the place
where i am at 90 degrees
and not 40

where is the place
when the eyes and ears open
and look ahead with some
vigor
not cowardly

my brushstroke's target
the through line
where north,
south
and
west
do not cloud

sifting into this field and its
nursery of wonders
in the half light
soft and blonde
sometimes (just) here
when all goes quiet
...east echoes

RAIN SONGS

upon me
sweet first lines
have landed

a soft soak feathers the branches
and the day reveals itself
variations in "G"

rain songs -
lush in layers
truth has a texture

so the question becomes
do i make a fair catch?

or, level down first light
press and compress
pursuing, never catching
then,
slump stumped in evening for coming
short

"Life
Be still - be still!
Boundless truth is shattered
On thy hurrying current."

the magic flutes
out my window
still they nod
in soft sifts through the oaks
as i, for a moment
**allow astonishment to
  pause me**

can i
**can i accept
morning's blessing**
be blessed

just what will it
take to befriend
the bridge
to get to...

**YES
?**

pour light

show us your pastels
make us wonder
there is no picture that is wrong

there are rhymes draped
among
the thorns
so, what
what for you is poetic?

walking on the sand in
moments without time
i make blue pictures
in my mind

who is the painter,
where is the sun,
what do you know?

we are the unprimed
canvas
onto which the elegant
spills and soaks

see what it is
pour light
there is no picture
that is
clumsy

STEADY ROCK

"HERE IS WHAT YOU HAVE TO DO,"
INSTRUCTED THE BOY
TO HIS SISTER
LATE AFTER NOON
AT THE CURBSIDE,
OF THE PASSING TRAFFIC

"YOU FIND A STEADY ROCK."
"AND, YOU JUST SIT THERE."

AND SO FOLLOWING HIS RECIPE,
SHE TOOK A SEAT . . .
ON HER STEADY ROCK
AT THE CURBSIDE,
OF THE PASSING TRAFFIC
LATE AFTER NOON

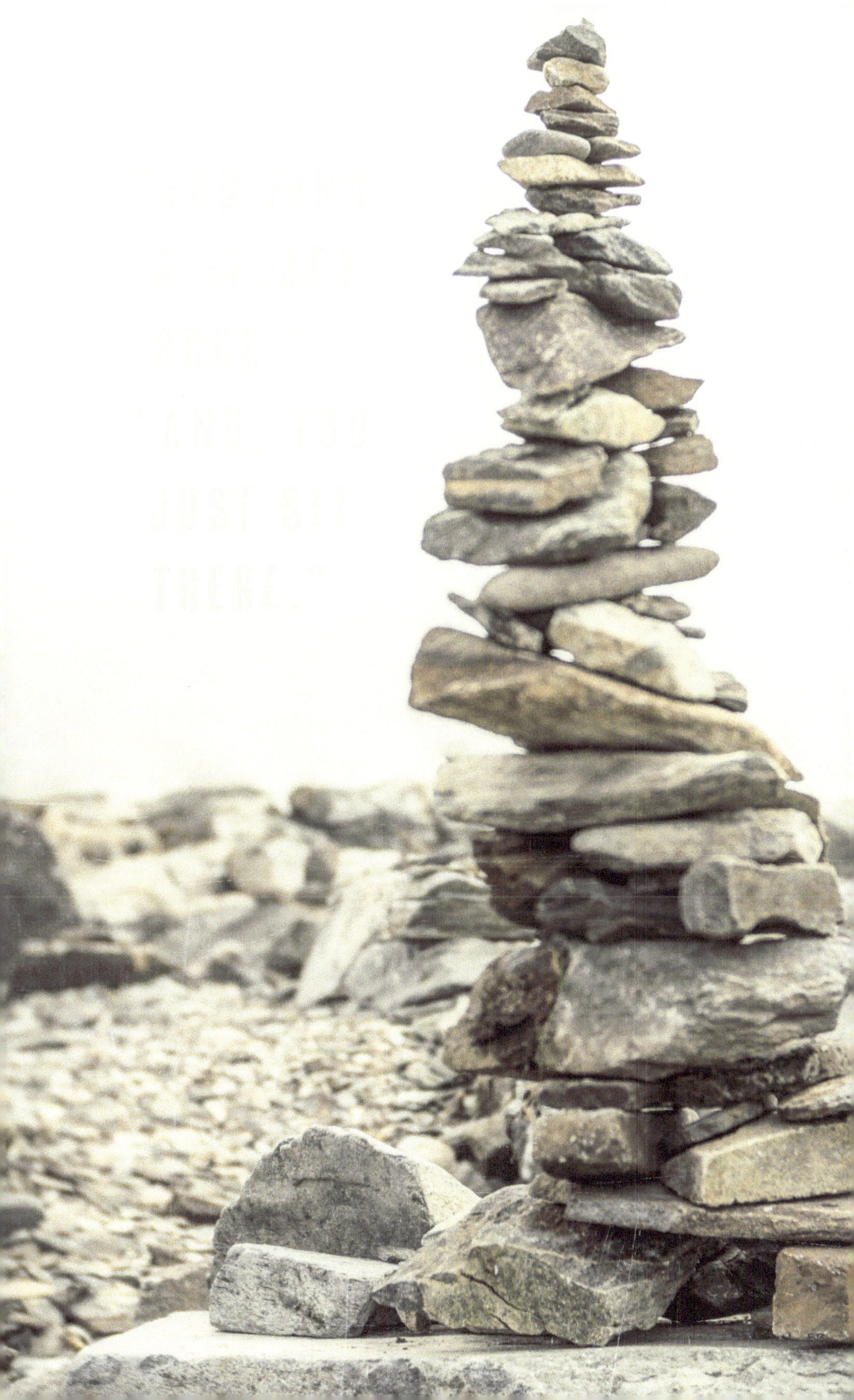

breathtaking

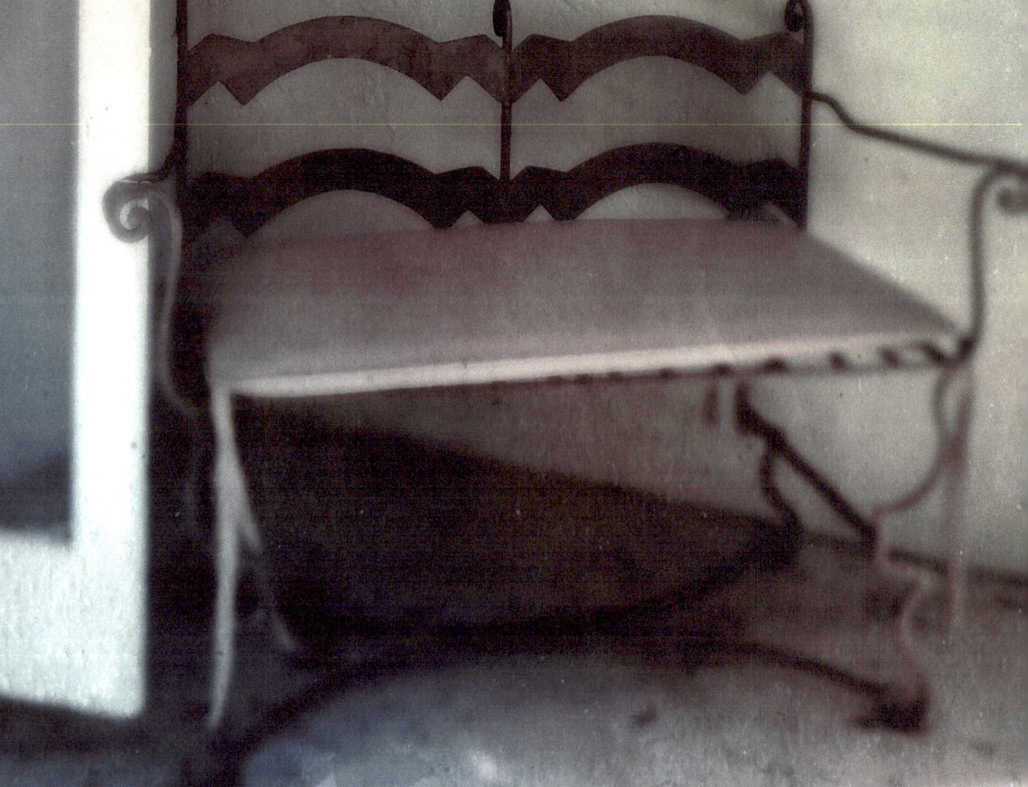

p

a

u

s

e

the chain

a few sighs out
lead to now
now leads to here

in staying put comes a clearing
like the forest interior when the
shimmer finds its way in
and presses over and in and through
deep shade

in the clearing with truth i am aligned
i am the pine, the mountain,
the confident current

truth insists on practice
keep the light lit
the 200 step process

the wheel spins
waking up
showing up
showing up
waking up
then, the one i seek

ah, my notes
breath breathes me
soul sings me

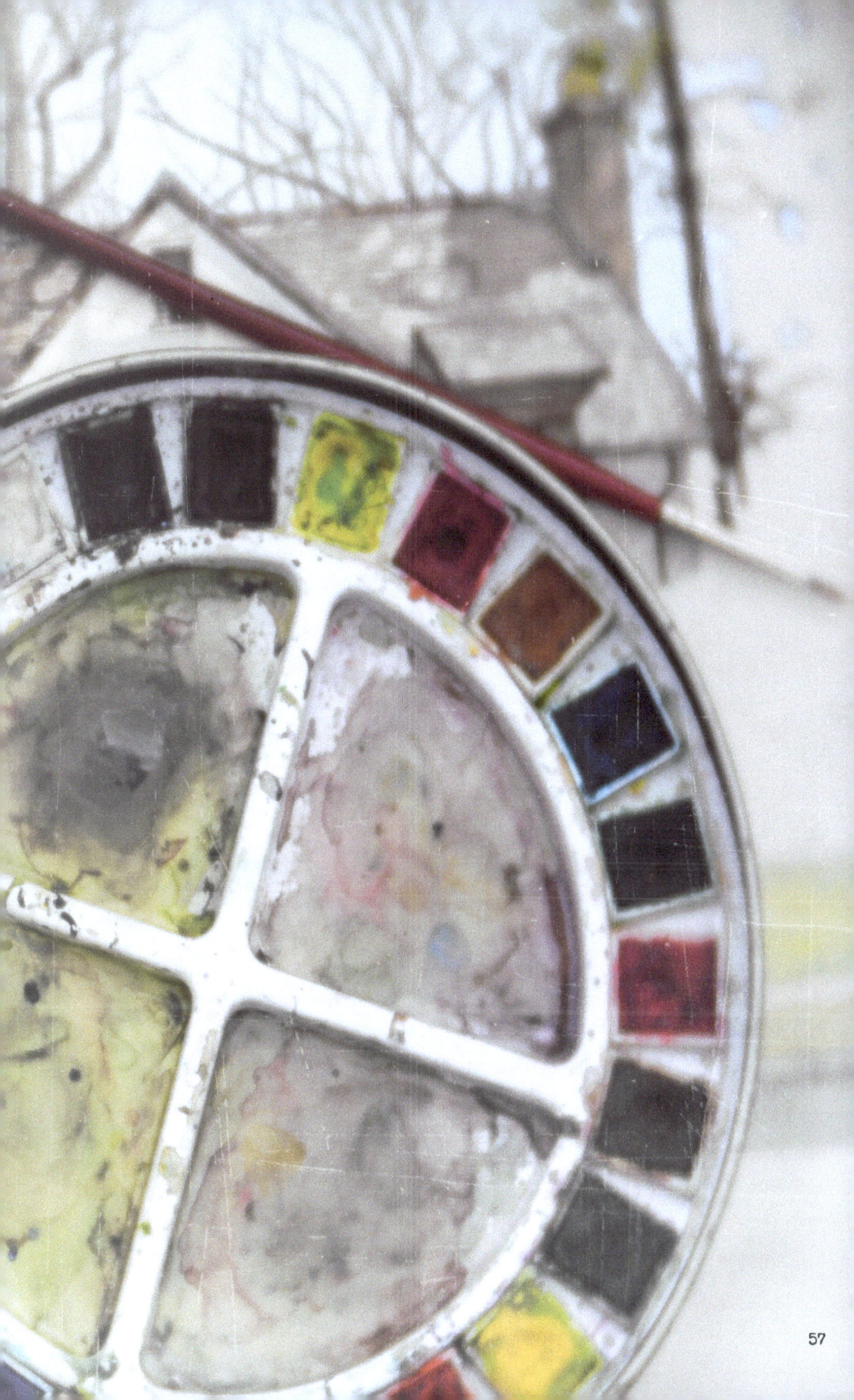

private practice

i'll take the day mild
and break it in silence
gathering pieces
of me

"the lighthouse
invites the storm
and lights it."

when i make perfect the quiet,
some things which visit are:
moons
stars
radiant beams
bliss

it hurts going in
gathering pieces
and finding
...the warrior

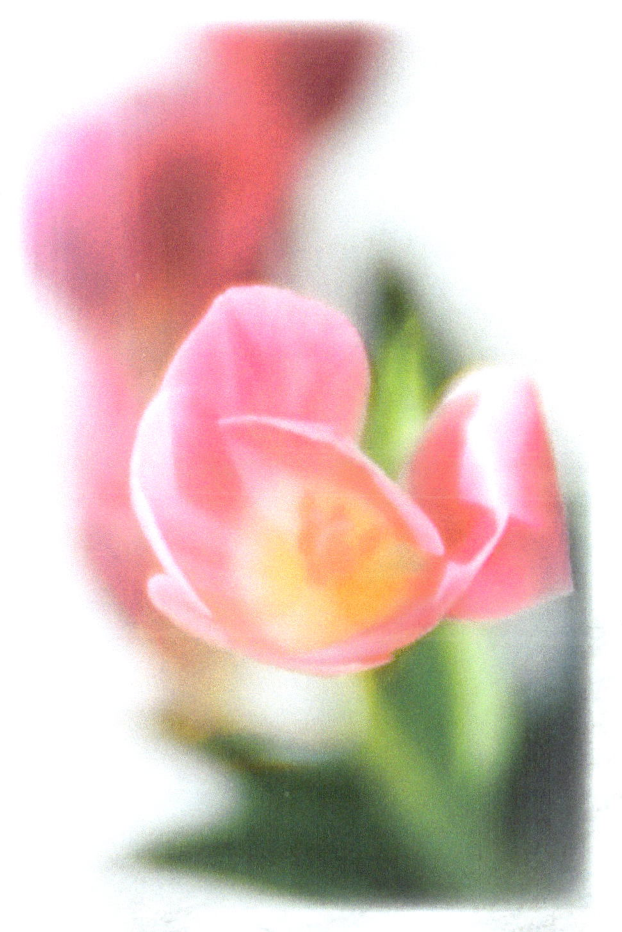

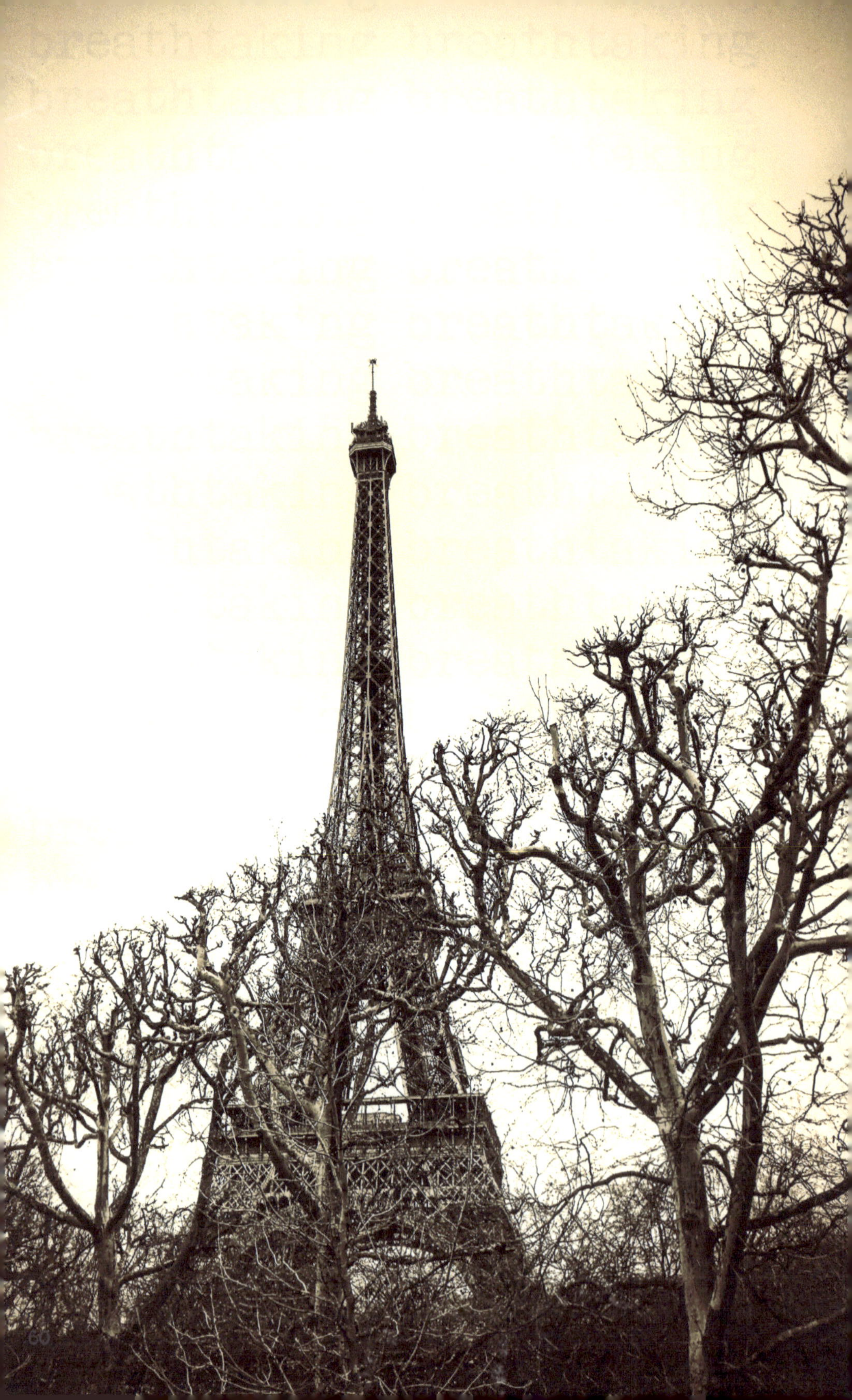

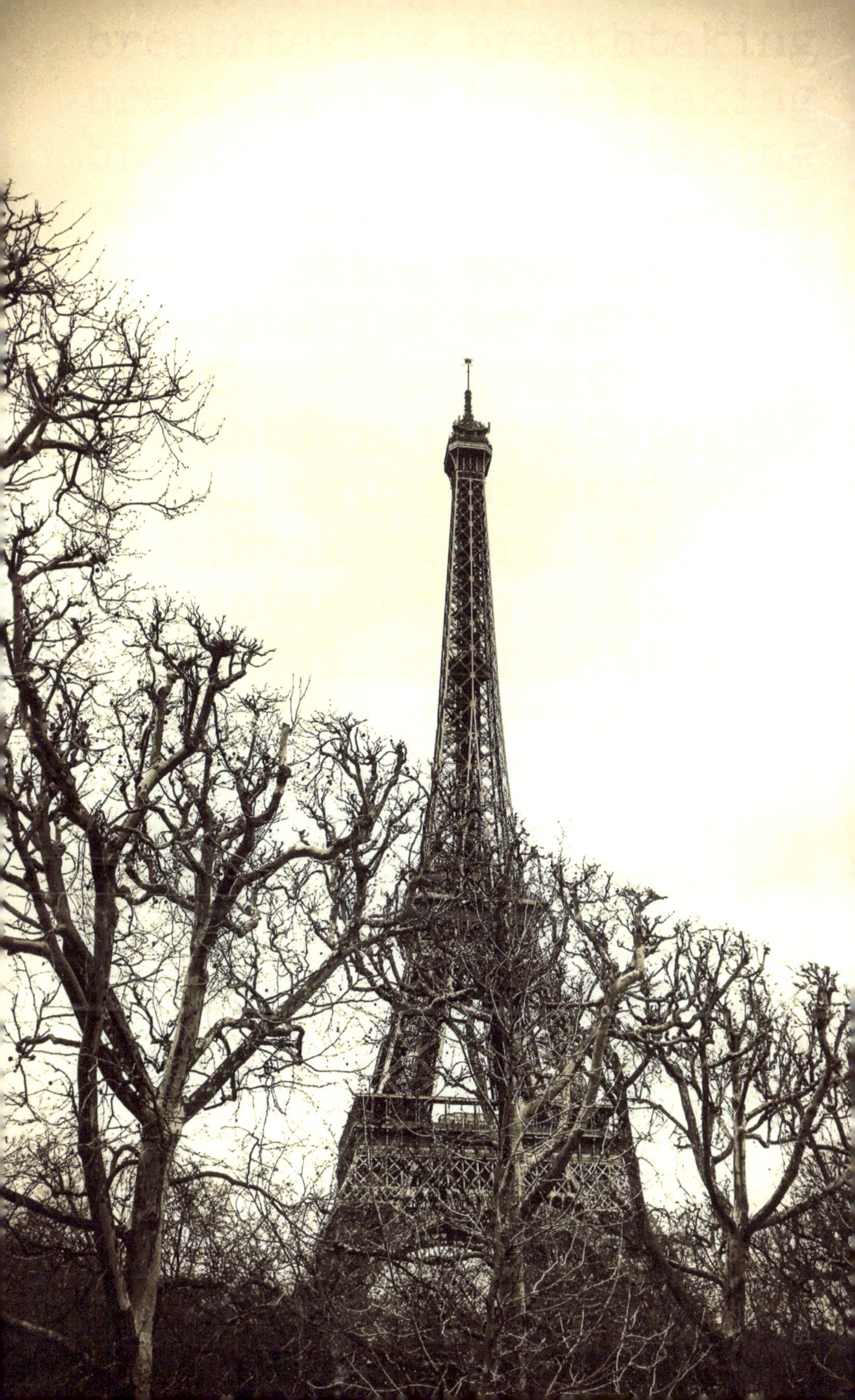

in the gradient

"make the hands beautiful," she instructs

slight shifts
and adjustments
and edits
in order to bend
bend around the changing weather

and then i arrive at today's definition
of lovely
where there's not a thing that i would
change

if anyone asks,
tell them i am mixing gray values
moving in shades
giving motion to something static

reminiscent of the painters
the canvas their neutral,
and with their angular gradients
misting off the rigidity

looking both inside and outside
of myself
making the shape of my own story
where **i can go anywhere**

suite for trumpet and strings

ever precisely
bowed instruments sing
and the one, just the one
french horn
pipes back

mirror, mirror
and so it goes
over keys and notes
the strings calling each play
the understudy building the
muscle
water suites

somewhere
the movement is mastered
and all join forces
striking together
in D

water suites
and a grasping
of unison,
of things arranged to be
played as one
and devotion
in D
or, in other keys

the comma

east of this marker
i will pivot
likely . . .

i will pivot back to habit
and scattered ways

but,
on a january friday
this comma
permits me to gather
to gather, and recalculate

destinations . . .
i'm weighing the energy
we expend to their plotting?
and, how it deflates

in the reserve
and my bask in it,
i'm bowing to
punctuation

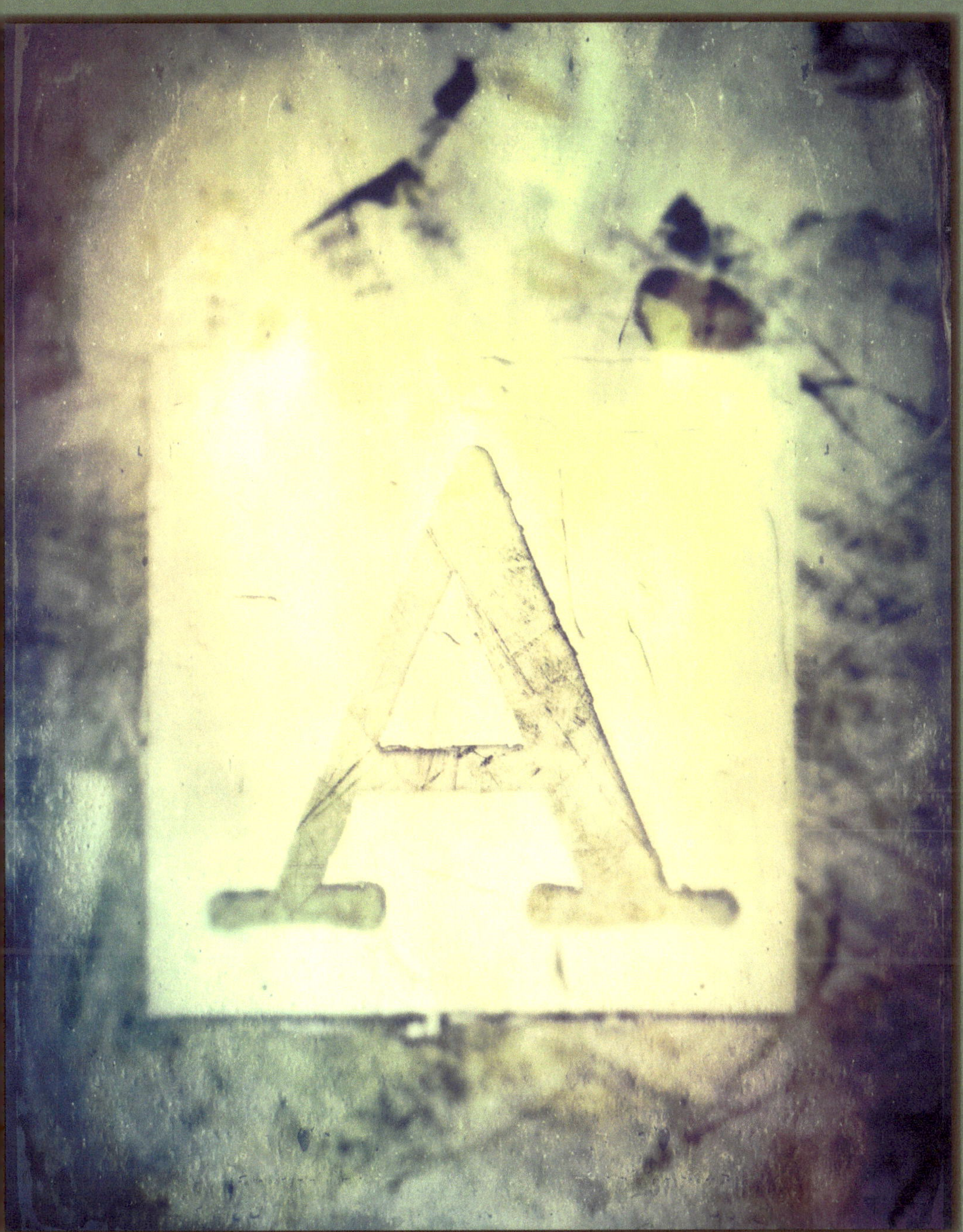
A

LIGHT THREADING

ONE DAY WE WILL ALL
LOOK BACK AND
REALIZE IT WAS JUST THREADING
LIGHT

ALL OF OUR HOUSEKEEPING
  JUST BEAMS
SLIPPING IN AND SLIPPING OUT
OF SHADOW'S MENACE

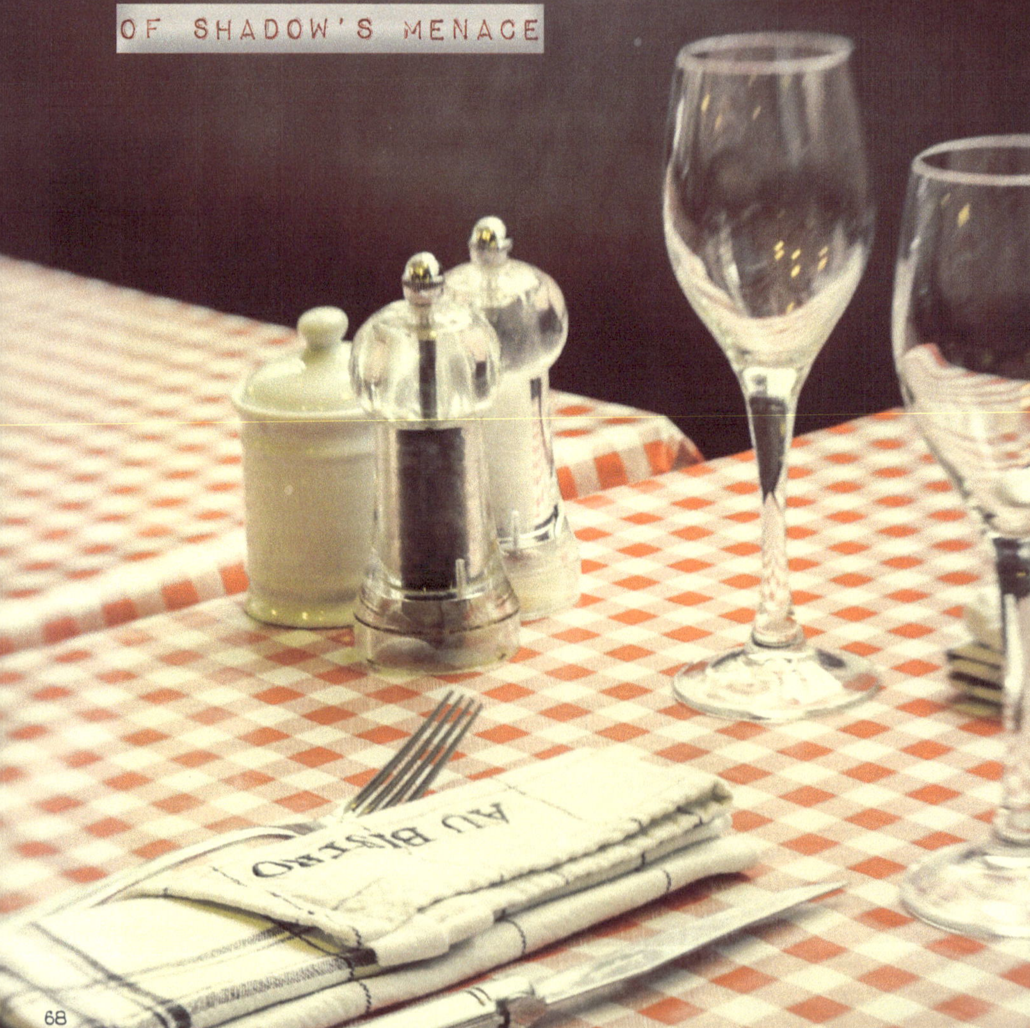

EACH MORNING
SETTING OUR TABLES
FOR ONE DIRECTION OR ANOTHER
AND THEN WAITING
FOR THE GUESTS TO ARRIVE

ONE DAY WE WILL ALL
UNDERSTAND THE PALE WEBS OF
DELICATE LINES
ELIMINATE THE NARRATIVE,
AND BE...
FREE

MIRRORING THE YOUNG GIRL
IN THE MASTERPIECE
AT THE PIANO
LIFTING HER RIGHT HAND
IN SPACE
THEN EVER SOFTLY FLOATING
INTO THE CHORD

ritual space

land in silence,
tap lightly
like the drops
of rain
ignoring today's soggy forecast

forward progress
. . . hold some back
let the quiet be the note
i hear the fellow with his trumpet,
his reply to shifting content

say what you mean to say
and only,
only that
thunder alone mucks up the voice

in ritual space
the measure, *or message*
will lull or pester
soothe or badger
only the architect can say

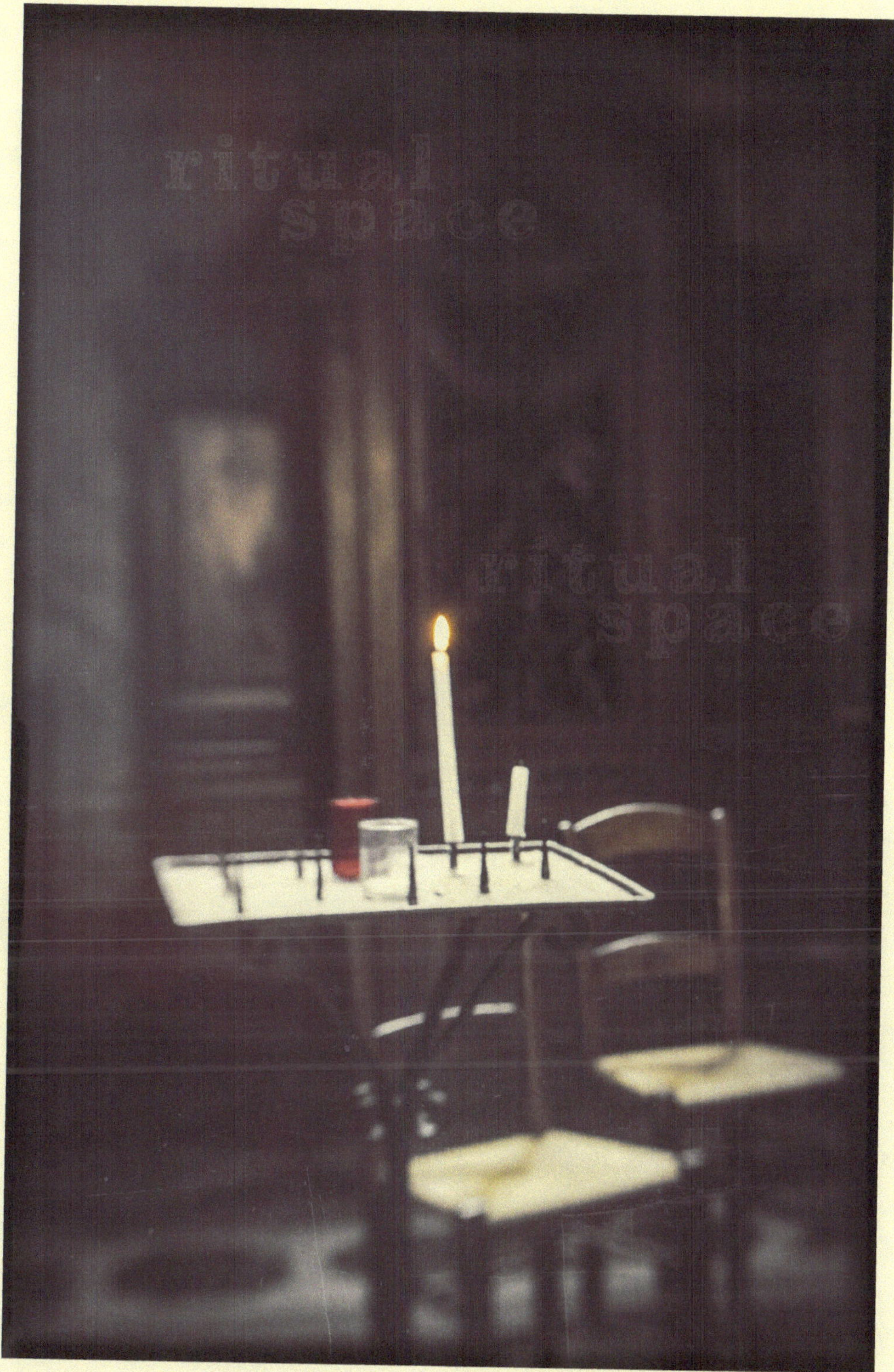
ritual
space
ritual
space

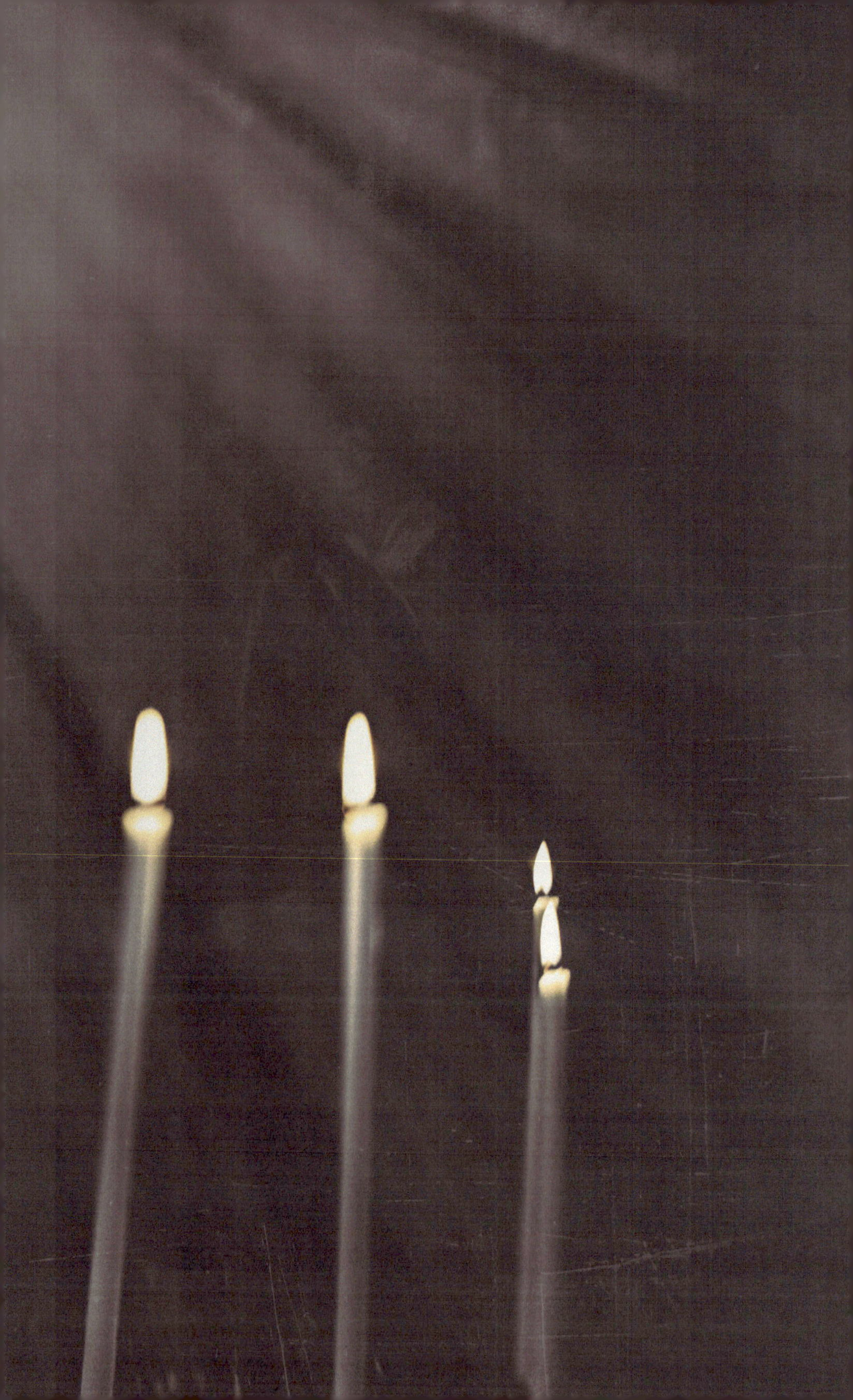

pause

to be swayed

the state of mind called "don't know"
we could all be wiser
in it

it would look like this . . .
you speak, i listen

i lean into your verse
with a willingness

to learn
something new
. . . to be swayed

not knowing everything
it would look like this . . .

a road not considered appearing
topography swelling
with each new teacher

the state of mind
called "don't know"

it could look like . . .

CLARITY,

EASE,

WONDER

. . . A BRIDGE

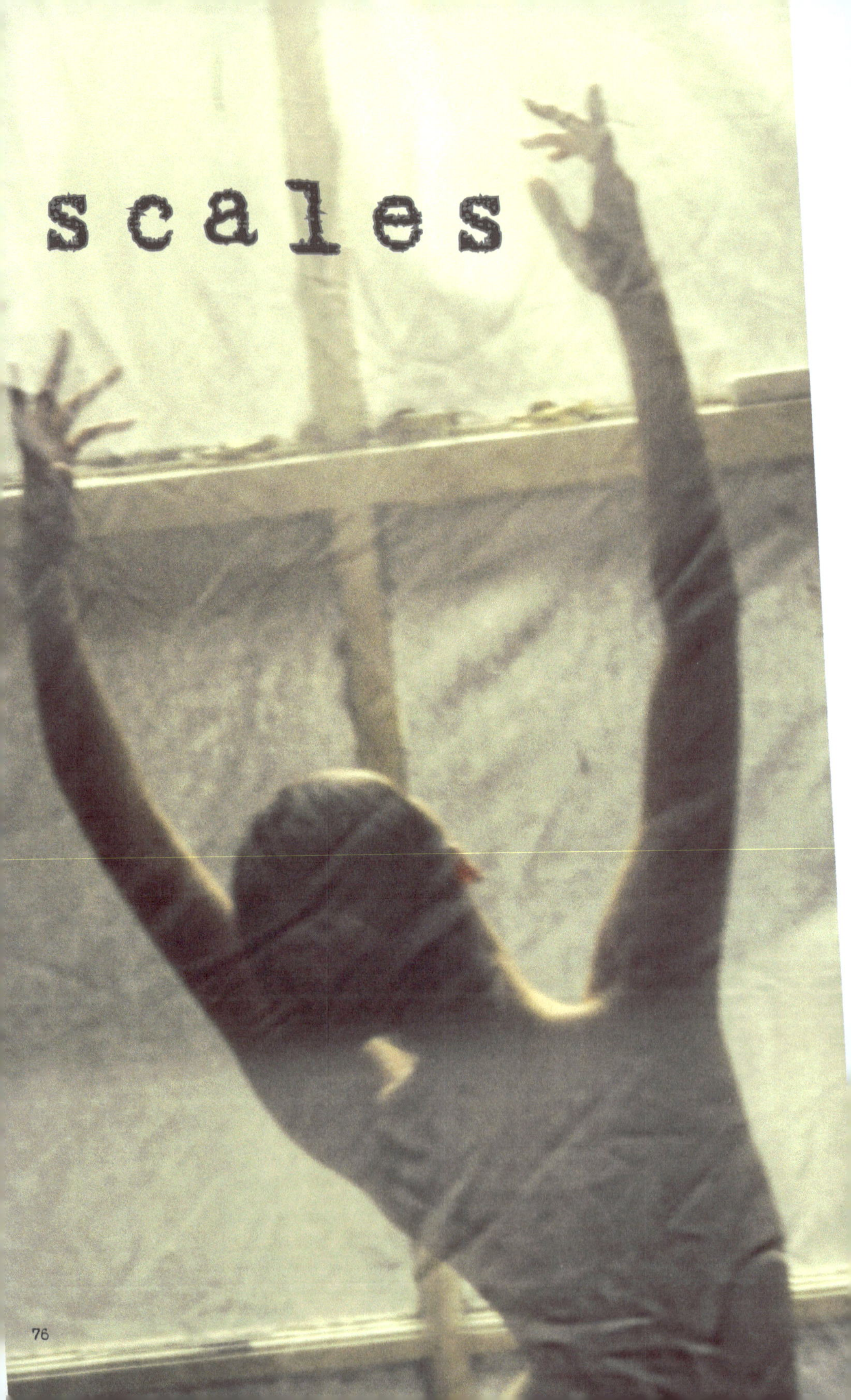

scales

as i recall the young girl in the
masterpiece
at the piano
lifting her right hand
in space

then melting into the chord . . .
i'm chewing on the question of scale

    what is heard
    what is seen
    and what
    remains invisible

ours is a time of tides . . .
the rush and the recede
to where

my incline is towards the suspension
the silver space
like the gap now at the day's edge
in the foothills,
with the sun in its silent
southwest descent
the clouds ghosting the horizon

and **my small figure just vanishing**
into evening

field trip

field trip

this is me,
if anyone asks

if anyone asks
tell them this,
tell them that i'm blinking
beauty
  back
stockpiling grace
with the truest lens i know

  i'm being overwhelmed
  by authority figures
  like the late autumn half
  light
  as it dusts the pasture

soon the day will be no more
but, for these few fading
moments

there are punctuation marks to honor
. . . the shimmer of the chipped bark
and, the golden flutter as it mirrors
what is left

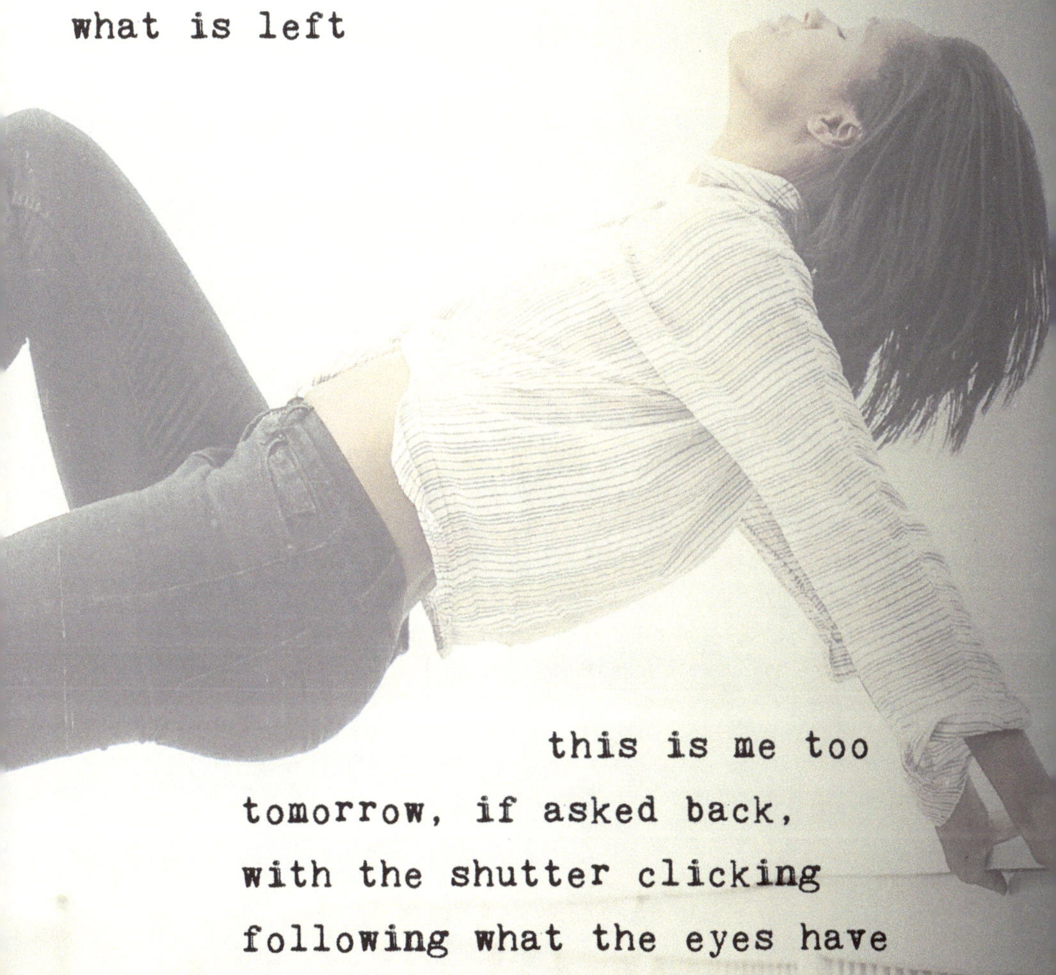

this is me too
tomorrow, if asked back,
with the shutter clicking
following what the eyes have
again blinking beauty
back
into the open

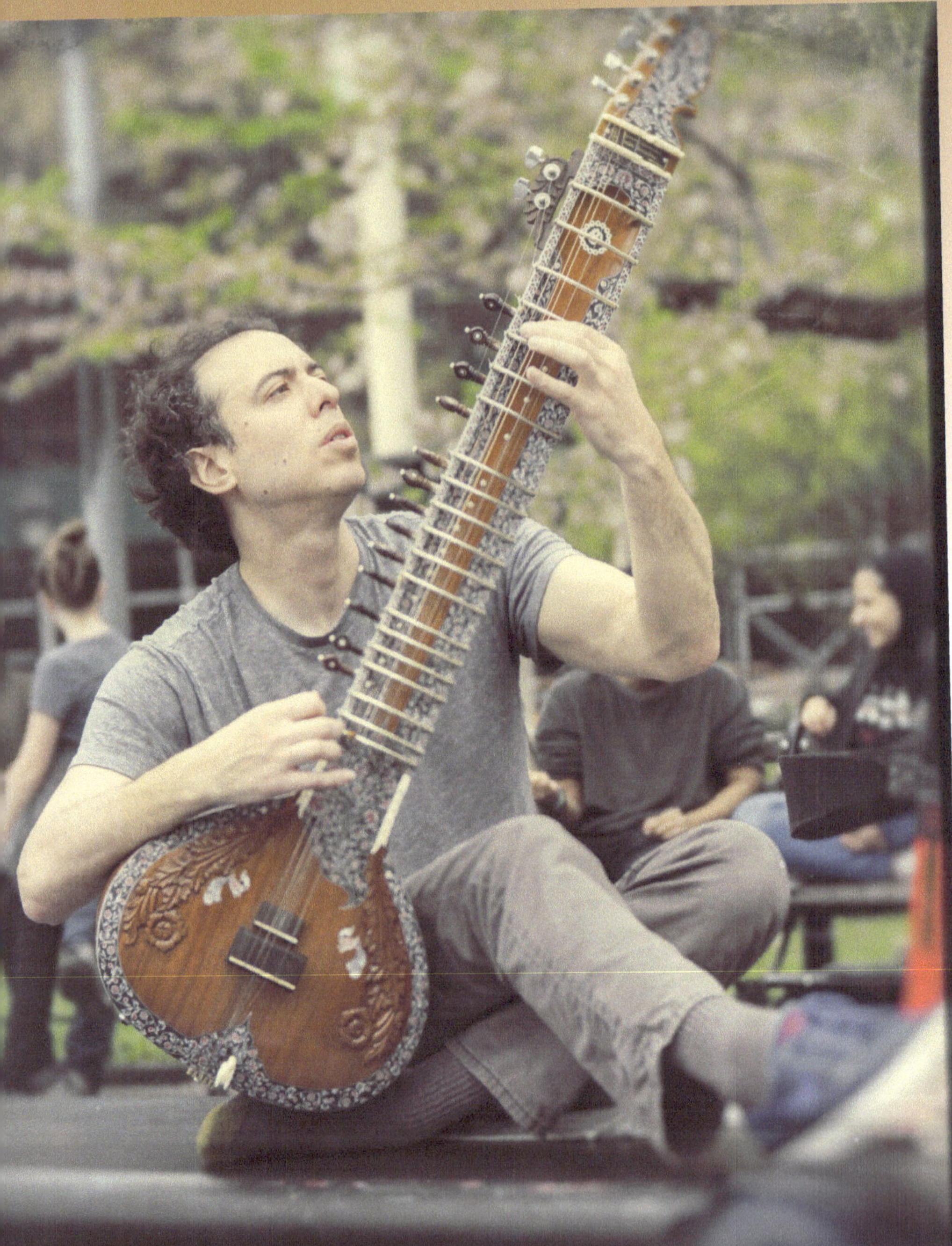

HEAVENLY REACH

the cathedral, the cathedral
never lose its sight

on with the art game
the words, the pictures
the whistling in dimly lit rooms

ever at it,
and ever again
charged with the fancy
that one day . . .
pews will be occupied

on with the heavenly reach
ever at it,
and ever again
certain that one note, or two
may transmit
or not

the cathedral, the cathedral
where the pipes sound and in filters
the sunlight
for all eyes, for all ears

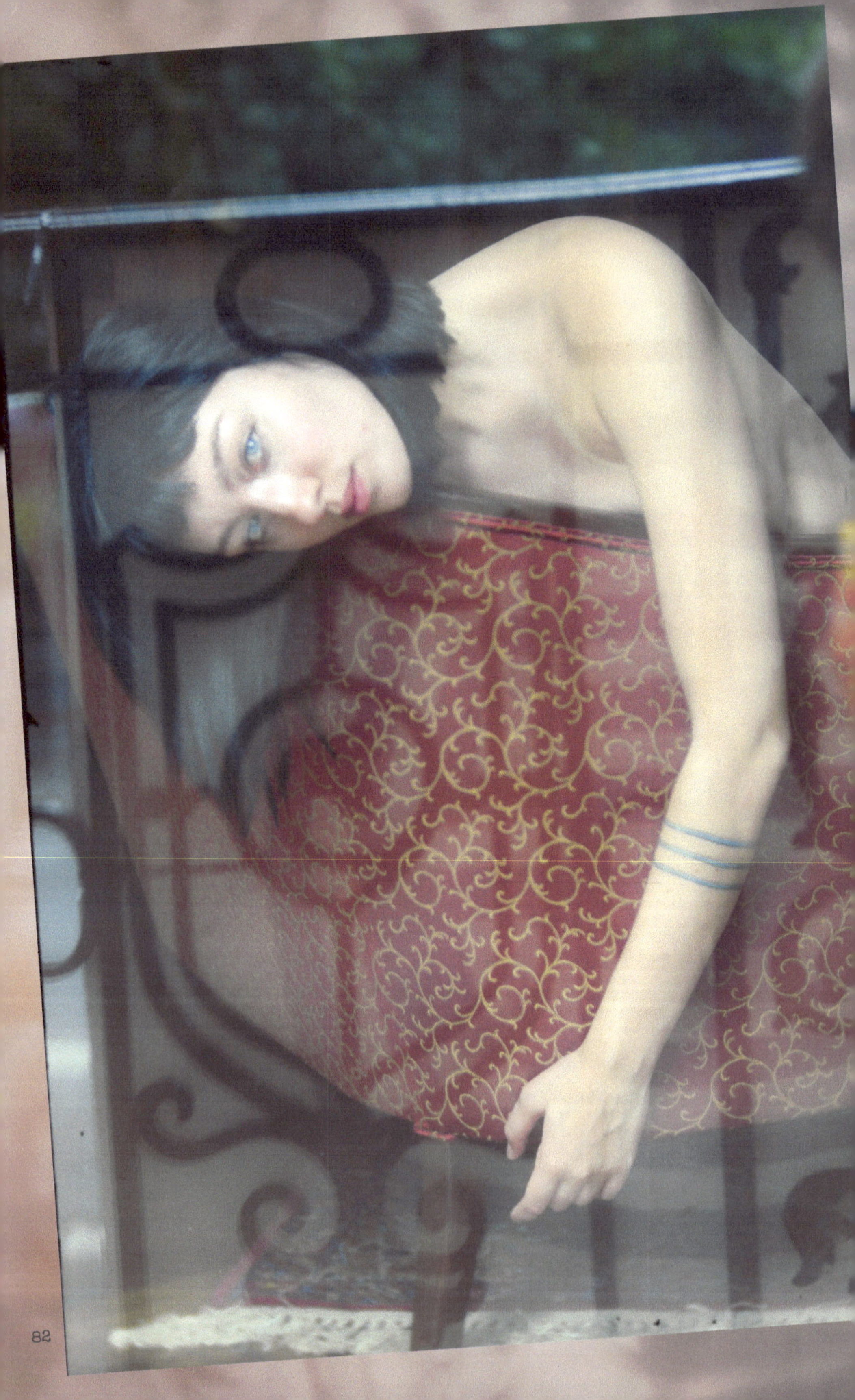

shadow cuts

a greater version of me . . .
it exists within
some where
so i sit, still
to unwrap the sluggish one

still, but fluid
quarrying space,
and time

still, but expanding
inching closer
in body, in heart
. . . in mind

to dwell unhindered like the breeze
not caught in a net
shadow cuts,
and this could happen
to me?

"sit still," it was ordered
but never coached how

as the chilled pines do
so precisely
on the shortest day

inhale exhale

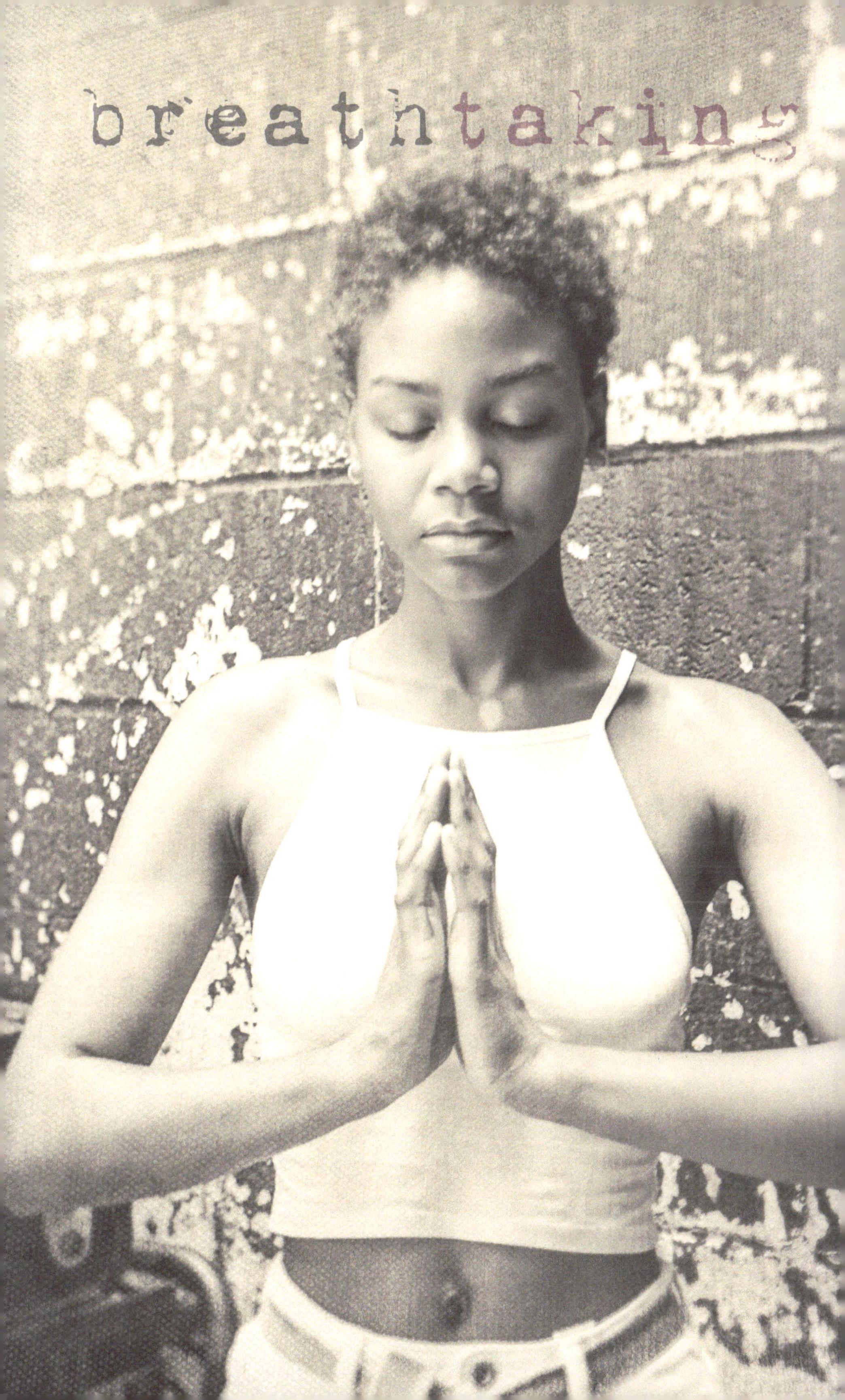

breathtaking

show notes

then the backlit field
peach before november
summons me

fading into analogue
i go for the long view

"une vie tranquille"
the notion of such
arises

sweeps its shawl over me

i go for the long view
and the only progress
is the record

. . . the record i am making
with ears and eyes and lungs

of this unearned ease
brought to me by . . .

standing still among the trees

not yet leafless

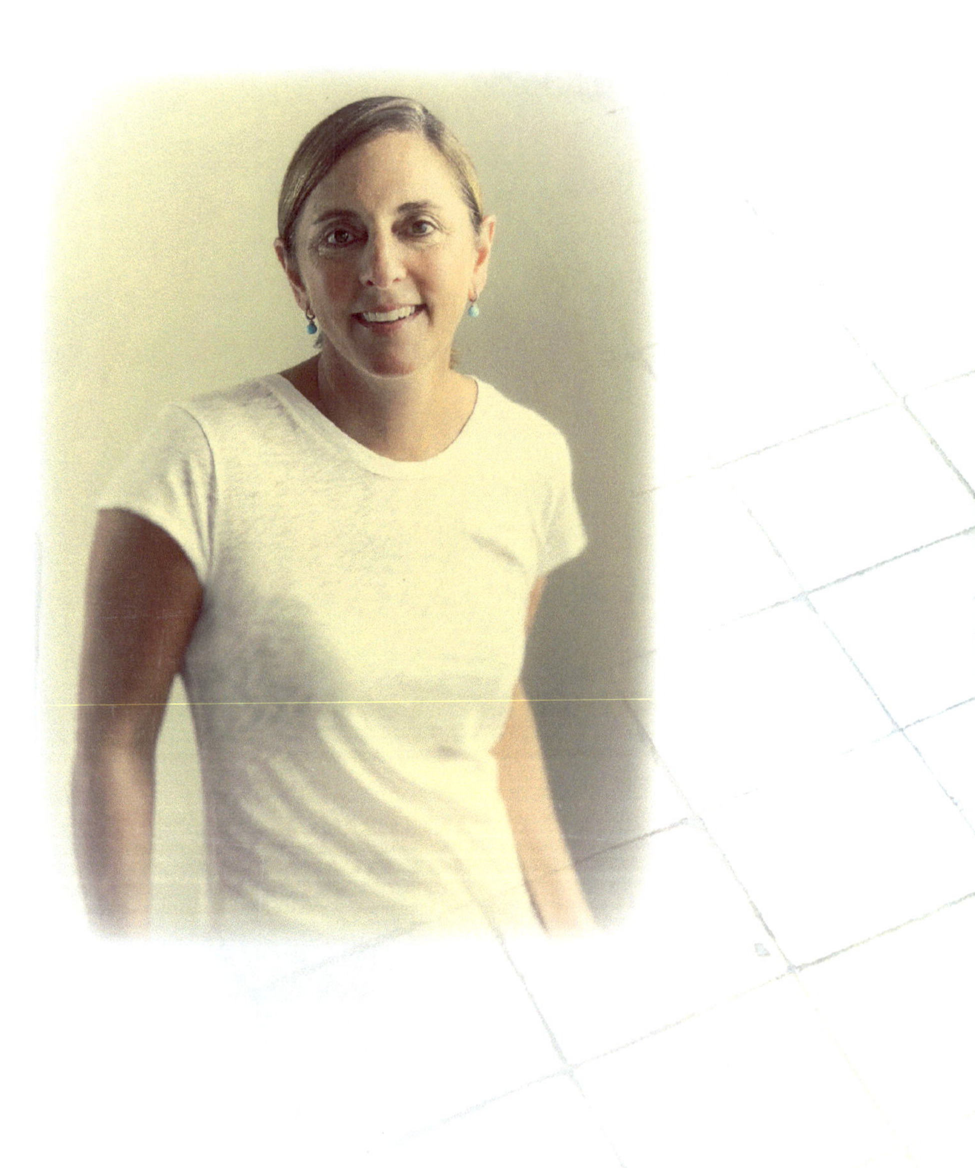

susan currie is a west palm beach based photographer and writer. her words and images have been on exhibit throughout the country and featured in *the boston globe, l.a. yoga magazine, we are travel girls, still point arts quarterly, the tishman review, temenos literary journal* and assorted other publications. currie is also the author of once divided (shanti arts, 2016) and its follow up, GRACENOTES, released in 2017. susan met her muse when she discovered the practice of yoga (and became an ryt 200 instructor) some time ago. this ancient eight-limbed practice continues to inform her artistry and her life on a number of levels. through the creative workshops she leads throughout the country, she shares her signature approach to slow shooting and incorporating mindfulness into the artistic practice.

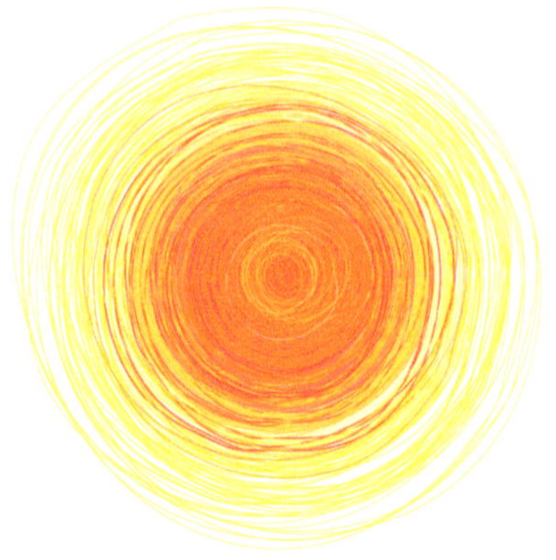

www.ingramcontent.com/pod-product-compliance
Lightning Source LLC
LaVergne TN
LVHW052307100826
845147LV00006B/698

* 9 7 8 1 9 4 7 0 6 7 9 1 2 *